Praise for *Inside*

"*Inside the Schoolhouse* will serve as an essential resource for any new principal, or for any instructional leader looking to get into school administration. The contents of this book provide principals with a road map to success and will serve as a constant reference for them every step of their journey. As a division leader, it is essential to offer trustworthy support to our school administration, and this book will certainly become a new and powerful support for our leaders." —**Scott L. Jefferies**, EdD, superintendent, Wythe County Public Schools, Virginia

"The wealth of knowledge and experience Dr. Gratto brings to *Inside the Schoolhouse* will help aspiring, new and experienced principals alike hone their craft, aiding them to become even stronger school leaders than they currently are. This text would be especially useful in principal preparation programs, as we work to develop strong, competent leaders for the schools of the future. School divisions could also benefit from the information in the text when working with newly appointed administrators, guiding them through the best practices for instructional leadership based on both solid research and practical experiences. I highly recommend this text, and Dr. Gratto, without reservation." —**Michael D. Kelly**, EdD, principal, Frank W. Cox High School, Virginia Beach, Virginia

"*Inside the Schoolhouse* is an excellent resource for educators considering a school leadership role or for experienced principals looking for practical guidance. For example, chapter 1 notes the value of consistently asking 'whom do you serve' when making decisions involving faculty, staff, and parents. Knowing that students are the focus makes navigating different constituencies more straightforward and manageable. This book presents practical information and thoughtful questions that inform critical decisions with regard to building a quality school." —**Jeff Nichols**, superintendent of Schools at Sag Harbor (NY) School District and twenty-year high school principal

Inside the Schoolhouse

Inside the Schoolhouse

What Great Principals Know and Do

John Gratto

ROWMAN & LITTLEFIELD
Lanham • Boulder • New York • London

Published by Rowman & Littlefield
An imprint of The Rowman & Littlefield Publishing Group, Inc.
4501 Forbes Boulevard, Suite 200, Lanham, Maryland 20706
www.rowman.com

6 Tinworth Street, London SE11 5AL, United Kingdom

British Library Cataloguing in Publication Information Available

Library of Congress Cataloging-in-Publication Data

Names: Gratto, John, author.
Title: Inside the schoolhouse : what great principals know and do / John Gratto.
Description: Lanham : Rowman & Littlefield Publishers, [2021] | Includes
    bibliographical references. | Summary: "This book addresses the most common issues
    faced by new or veteran principals"— Provided by publisher.
Identifiers: LCCN 2021000860 (print) | LCCN 2021000861 (ebook) | ISBN
    9781475855678 (Cloth : acid-free paper) | ISBN 9781475855685 (Paperback : acid-
    free paper) | ISBN 9781475855692 (ePub)
Subjects: LCSH: School principals—United States. | Educational leadership—
    Standards—United States. | School management and organization—United States.
Classification: LCC LB2831.92 .G72 2021 (print) | LCC LB2831.92 (ebook) | DDC
    371.2/012—dc23
LC record available at https://lccn.loc.gov/2021000860
LC ebook record available at https://lccn.loc.gov/2021000861

∞™ The paper used in this publication meets the minimum requirements of
American National Standard for Information Sciences—Permanence of Paper
for Printed Library Materials, ANSI/NISO Z39.48-1992.

Contents

Preface

One year while I was a principal, I also moonlighted on weekends as a limousine driver. One night, I picked up an executive who had flown into town to open a store. He told me that, as a top executive of a national chain of restaurants, he went all over the country to hold ribbon-cutting ceremonies for new stores. As I drove him for a couple of hours, he asked what I did for a living when I wasn't driving limousines. I told him that I was a principal of a K–12 school. "Wow," he said. "I make a lot of money but I really don't do anything that matters much. You do such significant work. I'm envious of you."

He was right, at least about me. I was fortunate to be a principal, perhaps one of the most significant occupations out of all possible positions. My ongoing efforts helped teachers to examine their teaching strategies and improve upon them. From a quantifiable perspective, I am pleased to say that my collaboration with teachers resulted in increased achievement results for students. Beyond that, my many conversations with students who behaved inappropriately helped them to make better decisions. Those comments could likely be made by many, many principals. It is hard to think of a more significant job than being a principal.

Not only was it tremendously significant, it was also fun. My daily interactions with students and teachers were a constant source of interest and satisfaction. Fun at work is not an oxymoron. I can truthfully say that my work as a principal was greatly enjoyable.

I don't mean to make myself sound special or especially talented. I wasn't. The fact is, such meaningful, life-changing work is common to all principals. Being a principal is simply that type of position. Principals have the potential to strengthen the skills of teachers, transform the lives of students, and improve their entire school-community. The work of a principal is extremely challenging, highly enjoyable, and always interesting. Typically, the hours are long and the work is intense. I can't think of a more satisfying job.

To further emphasize the importance of principals (and why the information in this book is important), here is what the New York State Education Department stated about the role of the principal in a workshop that I went to in my first year as a principal:

> The principal is potentially the most important and influential person in any school. The principal's leadership sets the tone of the school, the climate for learning, the level of professionalism and morale of teachers and the degree of concern for students. The principal is the main link between the community and the school. The way the principal leads largely determines the attitudes of students, parents and community toward the school.

Later, as a superintendent of schools, I worked closely with dozens of principals. As I collaborated with them and supervised them, the principles and strategies espoused throughout this book helped those principals to strengthen their skills and effectiveness. But the learning did not all originate from me; many of those principals were very talented and practiced highly effective strategies that helped me become a more effective coach and supervisor of principals.

I am now a professor of educational leadership and stay current with educational research and the many successful practices advocated by the numerous professional organizations that facilitate the work of principals.

I was asked to write this book after having had several articles published in *Principal Leadership*, the magazine of the National Association of Secondary School Principals. Apparently, the publisher thought that I could offer additional information to principals to help them do their important jobs more effectively.

As I thought about that request to write a book about strategies to help principals be more effective, I realized that I thought I had a lot to offer. Throughout my years as a school administrator, I learned many successful practices based upon solid philosophical principles, although not because I was ever a "Principal of the Year" or received any awards for my work. Rather,

I was much more like the thousands of hard-working principals throughout the nation who continually become more effective as we learn what works and what does not. There is some advantage in being experienced. I have learned a lot throughout my career as a school leader.

The result of all that I have learned in my own work as a principal, from working in partnership with principals as a superintendent, and as a professor of educational leadership courses is this culmination, this book, *Inside the Schoolhouse: What Great Principals Know and Do*.

The book is filled with far more practical, implementable strategies than theories. The principles and strategies explained throughout are grounded in proven practices that I learned in my twenty-eight years as a school leader and in my ongoing work as a professor of educational leadership.

As I shared draft copies of chapters with current principals and superintendents to garner their feedback and ideas to strengthen my points, they made these illustrative comments:

> *Inside the Schoolhouse: What Great Principals Know and Do*'s proactive approach to educational leadership overflows with successful practices and leaves no leadership stone unturned. From discussions regarding productive meetings and retention of teachers to a template for yearly school improvement goals and ideas to maximize instruction, this book is a practical and logical guidebook for principals. Operations, discipline, communication—it's all there.
>
> Whether you are new to the role of principal or a veteran administrator looking to improve, this book is valuable and highlights all of the management areas that principals handle on a daily basis. I found myself scribbling notes in the margins and making a list of ideas for the upcoming school year. Give this book a read; your teachers, parents, and students will be glad you did!
>
> —Katlin Kazmi, middle school administrator

> It is my pleasure to highly recommend Dr. John Gratto's new text, *Inside the Schoolhouse: What Great Principals Know and Do*. The wealth of knowledge and experience Dr. Gratto brings to this text will help aspiring, new, and experienced principals alike hone their craft, aiding them to become even stronger school leaders than they currently are.
>
> This text would be especially useful in principal preparation programs, as we work to develop strong, competent leaders for the schools of the future. School divisions could also benefit from the information in the text when working with newly appointed administrators, guiding them through the best practices for instructional leadership based on both solid research, and practical experiences. I highly recommend this text, and Dr. Gratto, without reservation.
>
> —Michael D. Kelly, EdD, high school principal

Dr. Gratto's book, *Inside the Schoolhouse: What Great Principals Know and Do*, will serve as an essential resource for any new principal or for any instructional leader looking to get into school administration. The contents of this book provide principals with a road map to success, and will serve as a constant reference for them every step of their journey. As a division leader, it is essential to offer trustworthy support to our school administration, and this book will certainly become a new and powerful support for our leaders.

—Scott Jeffries, superintendent

Hopefully, the practical, straightforward advice and strategies advocated in this book will cause you to draw conclusions similar to these school leaders. It is my hope that this book achieves its intended result of strengthening the skills of principals so that they will lead their schools with wisdom, knowledge, and a great deal of effectiveness as they carry out their noble profession. May your work as a principal be filled with great success and significance.

Introduction

The chapters of *Inside the Schoolhouse: What Great Principals Know and Do* each focus on a specific topic which will help principals to be effective. This is a practitioner-oriented book. Chapters address common issues that principals face and offer numerous strategies to help them achieve the skills and attributes necessary to effectively master those issues. Collectively, the fourteen chapters are designed to help prospective and current principals develop a wide array of in-depth skills, strategies, and attributes that will help them to flourish as principals.

While it is not the primary intent of this book, the chapters will also help principals master all ten of the Professional Standards for Educational Leaders (PSEL) prescribed by the National Policy Board for Education Administration (NPBEA):

Standard 1. Mission, Vision, and Core Values
Standard 2. Ethics and Professional Norms
Standard 3. Equity and Cultural Responsiveness
Standard 4. Curriculum, Instruction, and Assessment
Standard 5. Community of Care and Support for Students
Standard 6. Professional Capacity of School Personnel
Standard 7. Professional Community for Teachers and Staff
Standard 8. Meaningful Engagement of Families and Community
Standard 9. Operations and Management
Standard 10. School Improvement

Professors of Educational Leadership courses whose focus is to help prospective principals master those standards will find it helpful that, following a description of each chapter (below), the relationship of the topic of the chapter to PSEL standards will be stated.

The book could be read in its entirety or readers could simply read chapters that have relevance to them. Professors of Educational Leadership courses might consider using this as a textbook for their courses. Similarly, superintendents of schools could use this book for a book study with their principals as a means of establishing high-quality, consistent work throughout school districts.

Each chapter of this book begins with a very pertinent quote which illustrates the urgency and significance of that chapter and closes with relevant "Questions to Consider."

Principals must be masters of many skills and possess an abundance of leadership attributes. Chapter 1 asks an important question, "How would you like to have you as a principal?" It identifies positive attributes that cause teachers, staff members, and students to want to follow the leadership of principals. (PSEL standards 2, 3, 4, 5, 7, 10)

Much information is appropriately written about the importance of principals being instructional leaders, but "Management precedes leadership." Making the ordinary things ordinary so that principals can spend their time on school improvement initiatives is the focus of chapter 2. (PSEL standards 3, 4, 5, 6, 7, 10)

Chapter 3, "Leading instructional improvement," gets to heart of the instructional leadership skills which principals should possess. In these times of insufficient funding for schools, it also offers "Ten no-cost, high-yield actions to improve instruction." (PSEL standards 1, 2, 3, 4, 5, 6, 7, 10)

Schools must continually improve. Yet, sometimes principals are unsure of how to lead improvement efforts. And, to make matters more difficult, their efforts are sometimes impeded by people who are resistant to change. Chapter 4 explains "A three-step process for improving virtually any aspect of a school." It also provides direction for principals to overcome the seven steps of stagnation with the success questions. (All 10 PSEL standards)

A top priority of principals, of course, is to strengthen academic achievement of students. In fact, since 2015, all schools in the nation are required to develop a yearly school improvement plan under the federal Every Student Succeeds Act. Chapter 5, "Crafting a school improvement plan," provides clear direction (and a template) for principals to make a school improvement plan while providing practical strategies to implement the precept that

"Continuous improvement consists of goal-setting and motivating teams." (PSEL standards 1, 2, 5, 9)

A recurring theme throughout this book is that principals accomplish their work and gain support for it by working in collaboration with others. A dozen practical ideas to do so are in "Leading effective teams: How to hold productive meetings," chapter 6. (PSEL standards 2, 3, 6, 7, 9)

As many principals know, there is a nationwide shortage of teachers. Chapter 7, "Creating conditions for success and retention of teachers," addresses actions principals can take to help teachers be successful and choose to stay at their school." Specifically, it provides eighteen strategies to create conditions for the success and retention of teachers. (PSEL standards 1, 2, 3, 4, 6, 7, 9, 10)

Virtually every school has them: People who have lost passion for their jobs; people who just go through the motions rather than doing their best. Chapter 8 provides readers with ten strategies for "Motivating the unmotivated: Getting teachers and staff members to do their best." (PSEL standards 2, 6, 7, 10)

Principals today are under enormous pressure to improve test results. Those efforts are made much more difficult when students have poor attendance. It is hard to teach students who are not in school and those students, predictably, often produce weak results. Chapter 10 is entitled, "You can't teach kids unless they are in school," and proposes "Ten high-yield strategies to improve student attendance." (PSEL standards 3, 5, 8)

Strategies to address student discipline issues are usually not taught in principal preparation programs. Yet students invariably behave inappropriately, thus squandering teaching time and consuming principals' time as those issues are addressed. Chapter 11, "Preventing and addressing disciplinary issues," provides principals with ten strategies to minimize time handling disciplinary issues so that they can "Free up time to be an instructional leader." (PSEL standards 2, 3, 5, 8, 10)

The quote which leads chapter 11, "Maximizing the use of your time: Time-saving principles and strategies," clearly emphasizes the need for principals to make every minute of their day count:

> He who every morning plans the transaction of the day and follows out that plan, carries a thread that *will* guide him through the maze of the most busy life. But where no plan is laid, *where the disposal of time is surrendered* merely to the chance of incidence, *chaos will* soon *reign.* (Victor Hugo, emphasis added) (PSEL standards 1, 2, 6, 9, 10)

Part of a principal's success hinges on the principal's ability to communicate well to internal and external stakeholders, yet many principals do not develop a well-thought-out communication plan. Chapter 12, "Communicating to build confidence in you and your school," offers a dozen "Proactive communication strategies" principals could use to gain support for their schools while simultaneously building credibility for themselves. (PSEL standards 1, 2, 3, 7, 8, 9, 10)

Conflict comes with the job of being a principal because so many people have differing viewpoints and priorities, but it can be minimized and dealt with effectively when it occurs. Chapter 13, "Master communication and you manage conflict," provides readers with "Tips for preventing and dealing with conflict." Specifically, it cites tangible actions principals can take to avoid conflict in the first place, offers suggestions on how to resolve conflict when it occurs, and recommends measures principals should take if the criticism of them is accurate. (PSEL standards 1, 2, 7, 9, 10)

Rather than focus on one topic and corresponding strategies, chapter 14, "Friendly advice: Ideas to help principals personally and professionally," will help principals in a different way than the other chapters. It simply offers good advice—the type of guidance related to the personal and professional attributes and actions necessary to make principals successful—which doesn't fit so neatly into the previous categories. As a wise, older, experienced, mentor gives advice to a protégé, this chapter is intended to share wisdom gained over the years that will help principals stay out of trouble and build skills to be successful. (All 10 PSEL standards)

Being a principal is a high-intensity, time-consuming, highly significant position with the potential to positively impact the lives of students and teachers as well as entire school-communities. There are many facets to it. It is the hope of this author and the intent of this book that readers may find much value and practicality in the many principles and strategies explained within it.

The late teacher and astronaut, Christa McAuliffe, is credited with saying, "I touch the future. I teach." That is an apt quote for those in the teaching profession. This is an apropos quote for principals, "I shape the future. I lead." May the knowledge you have gained from this book enable you to shape a bright future for the school you lead.

CHAPTER ONE

~

How Would You Like to Have You as a Principal?

Whom Do You Serve?

I've come to the frightening conclusion that I am the decisive element in the school. It's my personal approach that creates the climate. As a principal, it is my daily mood that makes the weather. I possess a tremendous power to make a staff member's or student's life miserable or joyous. I can be a tool of torture or an instrument of inspiration. I can humiliate or humor, hurt or heal. In all situations, it is my response that decides whether a crisis will be escalated or de-escalated and whether a person is humanized or de-humanized. (Haim Ginott)[1]

Why are you preparing to be a principal? Or, if you are already a principal, why did you become a principal? Chances are that you were a successful teacher who realized that you could make an even bigger impact by leading teachers rather than teaching the students in your classroom. In fact, that is quite true. As a principal, you have the potential to influence dozens of teachers and staff members and hundreds of students and their parents. Your work can even affect an entire community. The position of principal holds the potential to positively, or negatively, influence many lives—depending upon your skills *and* the precepts that you operate by.

Whom do you serve? The actions of principals flow from the answer to that question. Maybe you see the principalship as a stepping-stone for yourself to reach a higher position. In that case, you would make decisions that favor your career advancement. Sometimes principals believe they serve the teachers and staff. In that case, principals say "yes" to decisions to keep staff happy, sometimes at the expense of students. Perhaps principals believe they serve parents or taxpayers. Those decisions have repercussions, too, which are not always positive.

Therefore, it is important for prospective and current principals to have some bedrock principles to operate by, some deeply held philosophies that buttress their actions. Here are seven bedrock principles that are common to successful principals. The best, most judicious, and solid bedrock principle of them all is: *Make and frame decisions in terms of their impact upon students.* Principals make dozens of decisions, often on a daily basis. A principal will make many prudent decisions by following the bedrock principle of making decisions in the best interests of students. It is difficult to go wrong when doing so.

As a principal, the person entrusted to lead a whole school, you are a role model all of the time. Much like a coach of a sports team, the question is not whether or not you are a role model. You are automatically, inherently, a role model by virtue of the position you hold. The question, then, becomes, "How good of a role model are you?" What values, attitudes, beliefs, and opinions should one have to be a highly effective role model as a principal?

The next bedrock principle is to *treat everyone with dignity and respect*—all the time, even when you don't feel like it or have been disrespected. Be kind, friendly, and respectful to students, even if they behave badly. Do the same with teachers, staff members, and parents whose behavior is unsuitable.

As you deal with someone who behaves inappropriately, keep the focus of the conversation on the behavior of the person who acted wrongly. Not only is it the proper and upright action for you to take in your position as a role model, if you are rude, derisive, or contemptuous, the focus of the interaction will shift from someone else's unfortunate behavior to your disrespectful behavior.

Your chances of resolving a conflict or addressing inappropriate behavior in an effective way are much greater if you show understanding and respect than if you are callous, sarcastic, demeaning, or snarky. More often than not, people will treat you the way you treat them.

In addition to treating people well, *you must continually model a positive attitude*. It matters greatly. As the principal, you will find no shortage of problems to solve. One of the vexing aspects of being a principal is having to solve problems that you did not create. That comes with the territory. Nonetheless, you can approach the hard work and difficulty of being a principal with a positive attitude.

Keeping an optimistic, can-do attitude with a smile on your face is catchy. So is grumbling and complaining. In fact, your mood often sets the mood for the entire school. The more you model a cheerful disposition, the more your staff, students, and the parents you deal with will catch onto it. Smile. Whistle while you work. Laugh. Put a bounce in your step. Continually demonstrate a positive attitude.

Show that you are not only highly competent but that you are also a pretty nice person to work with. Keep reminding yourself that you are very fortunate to have a position that holds the potential to affect so many lives in such a beneficial and constructive way, despite the difficulties and challenges inherent in it. Continually approach your work with enthusiasm and a zestful attitude. Remember, you are a role model at all times.

There's more that comes with being a role model. To use a metaphor, the principal is much like the mother or father of the school. Just like children notice, and often model, the actions of their mother or father, students and teachers notice, and often model, the actions of the principal. Therefore, *consistently model the behavior you expect of others.*

Since your actions are continually observed, it is essential that the principal have excellent attendance. It is also essential that you have a strong work ethic. Arrive earlier and leave later than most staff members on a regular basis. Do classroom observations when you say you are going to do them. Turn in reports on time. Keep your word. Demonstrate grit. Work hard consistently.

None of those actions can be viewed as a revelation. Nevertheless, you will be surprised and pleased at the respect you garner just for doing your work consistently well. Moreover, if a staff member doesn't adhere to some of the aforementioned inherent responsibilities of working in a school, then you will have the moral high-ground to address those deficient behaviors because you continually acted as a role model.

Be consistent. It is your responsibility to be the same person every day, with every person, regardless of whether you are having a bad day or personal issues.

Realize that difficult issues come with the territory. As a principal you will feel uncomfortable at times. You will have to have uneasy conversations with people who behave inappropriately. Leadership is challenging. Those conversations will be easier if you develop relationships with people, genuinely listen to their viewpoints, treat people respectfully, and make decisions in the best interests of students. More strategies for dealing with difficult issues and people are explained in the chapter on conflict resolution strategies.

Continually build relationships with students, staff, parents, community. There is an old expression, attributed to Theodore Roosevelt, which still holds a lot of truth: "No one cares how much you know until they know how much you care." One's effectiveness as a principal is certainly enhanced through positive relationships with students, staff, and parents. Make no mistake, it is better to be respected than liked.

Following the actions espoused in this chapter and throughout the rest of this book will enable you to be respected but not necessarily liked. Some people may not like you simply because you are the principal. However, the actions of a principal can increase the likelihood that they will be liked and there is no downside to being liked. In fact, people will often be very cooperative with you if they like you.

Relationships can be built in a myriad of ways. Demonstrating a sincere interest in people, expressing honest appreciation for their work or accomplishments, and listening and responding to their concerns are all effective methods. More strategies for building relationships are in the chapter entitled, "Creating conditions for success and retention of teachers."

A principal should never be disingenuous. Instead, sincerely and consistently work to build relationships with everyone you meet. You may likely be familiar with the concept of an emotional bank account. Much like an actual bank account, in to and out of which deposits and withdrawals are made, people have an "emotional bank account" caused by interactions with others, particularly the principal. Positive interactions with people, such as inquiring about them, their interests, or their family, make deposits into that emotional bank account. Greeting students, teachers, and parents in a friendly, warm manner makes a deposit.

Telling students you missed them when they were absent makes a deposit into that emotional bank account. (It also helps to increase their attendance.) On the other hand, sometimes withdrawals are made from that emotional bank account when a student or employee is confronted about inappropriate behavior. Therefore, a principal can still be respected (and perhaps even liked) when a withdrawal is made, if sufficient deposits have been made to outweigh any withdrawals.

Explain the rationale for decisions. Principals will find it effective to create a culture where staff members are not only free but also encouraged to offer their opinions on issues. Such a culture enhances staff morale because staff feel respected. Frequently, there will be many conflicting opinions on the best course of action to take and the principal must make a decision, oftentimes without any clear consensus from the people affected by the decision. Decisions, based upon their beneficial impact for students, as wise as they may be, may not be enough to engender support for them.

A principal should never resort to positional power when making a decision. "We're doing that because I am the principal and I said so" causes bitterness and resentment and increases the likelihood of mere surface compliance with a decision. Teachers who feel disrespected and demeaned by the exercise of such arbitrary decision making will likely say "Okay" to a decision, then close the door to their room and ignore a capricious directive.

"Think-alouds" are a strategy often used by teachers in their classrooms to explain how they solved a mathematical problem or came to a decision. Using "think-alouds" is also an effective strategy for principals to gain support for initiatives. A principal could explain the rationale for their decision by saying something like, "I thought deeply about this decision and considered all of the perspectives offered by the teachers. As a result, I have decided to do . . . for these reasons."

Such a decision that demonstrates an understanding of diverse opinions and articulates reasoned thought about the issue is likely to be respected and followed even if it may not have been the one advocated by some people.

A final and exceedingly important attribute of principals is that they *continually lead school improvement efforts.* As you will read in the next chapter, "Management precedes leadership." But, being an effective manager doesn't encourage followership. *Leadership* compels followership. Principals who make school improvement an ongoing top priority will help teachers teach better and students learn more. That is the inherent work of principals. While doing so, they will also earn the respect of many people. Teachers, staff members, parents, and community members will admire principals who put intense, ongoing effort into continually improving their schools.

Why would someone want to have you as their principal? In short, LEAD so that others will want to follow. A good rule of thumb in that regard is to think of how your interactions with people will be perceived by the people you interact with. These six bedrock principles will help students, staff, and parents want you as their principal:

1. Make and frame decisions in terms of their impact upon students; they are people whom the principal should serve first and foremost.
2. Treat people with dignity and respect.
3. Continually model a positive attitude.
4. Consistently model the behavior that you expect of others.
5. Continually build relationships with students, staff, parents, and community members.
6. Explain the rationale for decisions.
7. Continually lead improvement efforts.

There are many more precepts that cause principals to be effective. Additional effective actions of principals will follow in subsequent chapters.

Questions to Consider

Do I consistently:

1. Make and frame decisions in terms of their impact upon students?
2. Treat people with dignity and respect?
3. Model a positive attitude?
4. Model the behavior that I expect of others?
5. Build relationships with students, staff, parents, and community members?
6. Explain the rationale for decisions?
7. Lead school improvement actions?

CHAPTER TWO

~

Management Precedes Leadership
Make the Ordinary Things Ordinary

Make a point to continually search for a better way of doing things, even when things are going well, to ensure that a better alternative has not been overlooked and to keep your creative talents in practice. (John Maxwell)[1]

Let's say it's the first day of school and you are the new middle school principal. Five hundred smiling faces walk through the door in the morning. Some of those students walk to school or are dropped off by their parents. Do they know where they should go when they arrive at school? Is someone assigned to supervise them? Will everyone know where all of their classes are? Two of the teachers called in sick this morning. Is there a procedure to procure substitutes on short notice? Did the teachers provide the subs with lesson plans?

Are there enough chairs in every classroom? Will all of the students get fed within the assigned lunch period? Who is supervising the cafeteria to prevent food fights? After lunch, someone pulled the fire alarm. Will everyone know the fire drill procedures? At the end of the day, do all the students know which bus to get on and how to find it? Are staff members supervising the loading of the buses to help students and prevent horseplay?

There are dozens of such logistical issues that principals must plan to make sure that the ordinary actions within a school day are, indeed, routine, rather than chaotic. This chapter will emphasize the essential need for principals to plan thoroughly to ensure that the school runs well and also to establish credibility as a leader. It will also offer some principles to be efficient and effective when making those plans.

The literature about the responsibilities of principals is replete with a redundant and appropriate theme: Principals must be instructional leaders. Being an instructional leader is an inherent expectation and requirement of being a principal. No one will ever be hired as a principal with the charge to simply maintain the status quo. Indeed, principals' marching orders will typically be to improve reading or math scores, increase passing and mastery rates on exams, enhance communication with students and parents, create a positive school culture, provide meaningful professional development, increase the graduation rate, decrease the dropout rate, ad infinitum.

Compared to the many articles and books about being an instructional leader, there are comparatively few articles about the necessity of doing an excellent job with the ordinary issues of building management. Nevertheless, first things must come first. Why would teachers and parents believe a principal could be an effective leader if the principal cannot get bus dismissal procedures working smoothly? Will a principal have any credibility as an instructional leader if there is chaos in the lunchroom?

This book will offer many ideas and principles about being an effective instructional leader. However, before spending time on instructional leadership skills, it is necessary to deal with the fundamentals. Management precedes leadership. A principal must devote plenty of time to making routine issues operate routinely. Once a principal develops thorough plans to make ordinary building operations function in a routine and effective manner, then minimal time has to be devoted to them. The result, therefore, is that the principal can devote their time to higher-level skills and tasks such as improving teaching and learning.

Much of this essential planning occurs in the summer before school begins. Other times available to principals to plan to make the school run smoothly might be during winter or spring breaks when students are not in the building. Planning for some events such as assemblies, field trips, and graduation occurs throughout the school year. Principals' time is valuable and planning time must be used wisely.

Several points are essential here in this chapter addressing how management precedes leadership. Above all, the principal must plan for all aspects of students' and staff members' days to go smoothly. Here is a list of some issues that a principal must prepare for:

- ALL safety drills, plans, and procedures
- Before school and after school supervision of students

- Bus dismissal and loading, including appropriate supervision
- Class change procedures and supervision
- Lunchroom schedule and procedures, including appropriate supervision
- Playground schedule and supervision
- Procedures for parents dropping off items for their children
- Procedures for parents who want to talk with teachers
- Schedules for teachers and support staff that allow maximum time for teachers to collaborate by grade level or subjects
- Expectations for employees to treat students, parents, and each other with respect and dignity
- Expectations for teachers to respond to parents' concerns in a timely manner
- Procedures to get substitute teachers and support staff
- Requirements for teachers to prepare and submit lesson plans in their absence
- Orientation of new employees and substitutes
- Assembly procedures
- Supervision for extracurricular events
- Building supervision and management for whenever the principal is not in the building
- Changes in schedules due to inclement weather
- Procedures for students to park their cars on school grounds
- Late arrival or early dismissal procedures

That is a representative list rather than an exhaustive list. Principals would be well-served to consider their own school and its particular needs. Plan to ensure that *all* aspects of the school will operate smoothly. Think of every recurring issue that must function smoothly, as well as everything that could go wrong, to ensure that all routine issues have a plan to make them operate routinely. Make plans to ensure that backup plans also work.

An old adage goes something like this, "How will you have time to do something over if you didn't have time to do it in the first place?" Time devoted to planning well, in the first place, helps to avoid time spent (and perhaps wasted) because something was not planned well.

How does a principal devise appropriate plans for all of these issues? If you're new to a school, do your homework well. If possible, ask for guidance from the person who held the position before you. If that person is not available, pick the brains of anyone and everyone who can help you make effective and efficient plans.

A common way of making such operational plans is for the principal to write all the appropriate plans, schedules, and procedures herself. There is merit in doing so because the principal can make plans exactly as she thinks they should be. For example, the principal may choose to assign a person with a very pleasant personality to greet students as they exit the school bus and enter the school. Or, the principal may want to ensure that the master schedule allows for teachers at a particular grade level to all be scheduled for specials (art, music, physical education, library classes, etc.) at the same time so that they have the opportunity to collaborate in professional learning communities.

People closest to the situation invariably know the problems and concerns in their area and, often, the solutions to those issues. So, if the principal decides to be the primary author of these various management plans, she would be wise to then show the schedule, plans, or procedures to the people affected by them. Listening to feedback from teachers and other staff members accomplishes three things.

Firstly, respect is communicated by genuinely listening to people. Secondly, those people affected by the principal's decision often can offer ideas or revisions to make a schedule work more smoothly. Finally, seeking the advice of people to craft quality plans enables them to feel connected to the plans, making it much easier for them to buy into the plans.

Another method of devising the multitude of necessary plans, procedures, and schedules is to delegate their creation to committees or groups of staff members who are directly affected by them. For example, a safety committee might be able to create safety plans that result in the most expeditious plans for student and staff safety. If the principal chooses to delegate the creation of plans, she will then want to thoroughly review them to ensure that they meet the needs of the school and all of the people affected by them.

Whether the principal devises plans or delegates them to staff members, there is a common theme, which is fundamental to helping ensure the effectiveness of such plans. *Involve people in issues that affect them.* As talented and conscientious as principals might be, they are still fallible. In addition, they are not as likely to know the ins and outs of situations as well as the people who work there every day.

Again, a principal who respectfully involves people in issues that affect them is likely to (a) engender respect by doing so and (b) make better decisions. So, it is wise to take the time to talk with teachers, secretaries, cafeteria workers, coaches, etc. to get their feedback on the effectiveness of the plans to make routine issues routine.

Finally, the principal will help to ensure the smooth operation of the school by continually monitoring and adjusting all aspects of school operations as necessary. Scrutinize practices and procedures regularly to try to find ways to make them highly effective, standard operating procedures. Truly, the principal is the "quality-control" person for the school, the person who makes sure that everything is operating at a high-quality standard. Time spent up front devising schedules, plans, and procedures with people affected by them will likely result in well-planned and well-executed plans that will minimize time spent revisiting them. Thus, the principal will have more time to be an instructional leader.

Rarely is a plan so perfect that it does not have to be revisited. Therefore, time devoted to continually monitoring and refining plans helps toward the end goal of making ordinary things routinely ordinary. That time spent on management issues results in time available for higher-order leadership responsibilities, enabling the principal to devote minimal time to building operation issues and maximum time to being an instructional leader.

Questions to Consider

1. Is there a written plan in place for every ordinary function of the school: safety plans, lunchroom supervision, teacher absences, assemblies, extracurricular events, etc.?
2. Are those plans easily accessible for everyone to read?
3. Do all employees, including substitutes, know and understand them? How do you know?
4. What noninstructional activities routinely consume the principal's time? What could be done to make those activities more routine so they take up less of the principal's time?
5. Have people closest to the situation been asked their thoughts about how to make routine operations function more smoothly?

CHAPTER THREE

~

Leading Instructional Improvement

Ten No-Cost, High-Yield Actions to Improve Instruction

> The key to making your students' learning experiences worthwhile is to focus your planning on major instructional goals, phrased in terms of desired student outcomes—the knowledge, skills, attitudes, values, and dispositions you want to develop in your students. Goals, not content coverage or learning processes, provide the rationale for curriculum and instruction. (Brophy and Wentzel, *Motivating Students to Learn*)[1]

McKinsey and Company's study entitled, "How the World's Best-Performing School Systems Come Out on Top" (Barber and Mourshed 2007, 16), attempted to determine why some school systems consistently perform well and improve faster than others. Significant in their findings, they note that "a school's results can never exceed the quality of its teachers," which is also a compelling reason for school principals to continually focus their efforts on increasing the instructional skills and effectiveness of teachers.

There is not enough time in a lifetime to read all of the books and articles regarding principals' responsibility for continually improving instruction so that students' skills will improve. This chapter cites ten high-yield actions regarding instructional leadership that principals can implement to maximize the instructional skills of teachers. None of these ideas cost money. They just take concerted, focused efforts by principals to pay big dividends on time well spent.

The points in this chapter should be viewed as fundamentals. Of course, any observer of sports knows that fundamentals are not always mastered or consistently carried out. Therefore, the following fundamental actions should be regularly reviewed to ensure they are in place and concentrated effort must be paid to them to ensure they are carried out well.

1. *Require that teachers teach from bell-to-bell and check for understanding.* Regardless of the talent of teachers, their effectiveness can be maximized if they spend a maximum amount of time on task. Requiring that students be in their seats before the bell rings to start the class is essential. A bell-ringer type of activity or short quiz at the start of class are effective strategies to get students to class on time, thereby demonstrating that lots of learning will be occurring in the class and it is important that students are there to participate in it.

Next, teachers could and should review the objectives for the class. Posting them on the board and reviewing them at the start of the class focuses the teacher, thereby minimizing the likelihood of spending too much time off-topic. More likely, though, it focuses the students on the importance of the upcoming lesson. The book, *Classroom Instruction That Works* (Dean, Hubbell, Pitler, and Stone 2012, 8) states that reviewing objectives can "connect the learning objectives to previous and future learning" and results in measurable student improvement. Clearly making that connection is one way of developing relationships with students.

Another advantage of reviewing the objectives of the lesson is that doing so gives teachers the opportunity to explain how the lesson will relate to students' lives. "Discussing how the information to be learned in the lesson relates to students' current lives and future aspirations is a very effective strategy for making the lesson meaningful. The more teachers can personalize the upcoming lesson to particular students' lives, the more relationships with those students can be built.

Checking for understanding may be even more important than teaching from bell-to-bell. Checking for understanding throughout the lesson and at the end of it is also an effective means of making lessons meaningful while simultaneously building relationships. If teachers begin the class by reviewing the objectives for the upcoming lesson by stating something like, "Today we are going to learn about topics A, B, and C," then it becomes easier to ask students how they meaningfully might apply topics A, B, and C in their lives.

In addition to making the lesson meaningful to students (which helps to build relationships), two other important things happen when teachers make the time to check for understanding. First, and very importantly, teachers can assess the extent to which students understand the information taught during the lesson. That feedback gives them the opportunity to reteach or reinforce information during the lesson. Secondly, teachers can use the information they get from checking for understanding to plan their next lesson and identify students who need additional support.

As principals coach teachers toward greater instructional effectiveness, they could share this strategy for checking for understanding. Many parents ask their children what they learned in school today. The common response is "nothing." Often, the lesson presented ends a few minutes before the class ends and the teacher does not want to go on to a new topic in those remaining few minutes. Or a teacher could simply build checking for understanding into the lesson by saying something like the following:"When your parents ask you this evening what you learned in school today, practice telling them what you learned about topic A, by explaining it to the rest of the class and me." Rather than letting students mill around for a few minutes at the end of class, that strategy could maximize instructional time and check for understanding at the same time. The same process could be used throughout the lesson and for topics B and C.

Some people might argue that teaching from bell-to-bell could inhibit teachers' opportunities to build relationships with students, emphasizing that strong relationships with students are essential if students are to respect teachers and the subjects they teach. Most would agree that talking with students about their lives and how course content can be beneficial to them is an effective strategy to gain their respect and develop rapport with them.

There must be a balance, though. Sometimes teachers complain that there is not enough time to thoroughly teach all the standards they are responsible to teach. Inconsistent with that complaint is the amount of precious class time some teachers squander talking about recent sporting events, celebrities, and any other number of topics unrelated to the class they are teaching. How, then, can teachers develop relationships yet maximize class time for instruction? What is the right balance?

Fundamentally, teachers must convey to students that class time, every bit of class time, is important. They must instill meaningful reasons for kids to show up on time and significant enough consequences to make it more attractive to arrive on time and be ready for learning when the class begins. Once students arrive to class on time, teachers must practice the aforementioned strategies of teaching engaging lessons and clearly relating those lessons to students' interests. Doing so will both build relationships and facilitate maximum student achievement.

2. *Ensure that all curricula are aligned to state and local standards.* That sounds pretty fundamental and it should be. But, sometimes it is not and that lack of alignment results in gaps in instruction and subpar results for students. Sometimes teachers teach what is enjoyable for them or a favorite unit they

have developed and enjoy teaching—even if those lessons do not align to the required standards.

Sometimes, teachers are not aware of the standards. That is more likely true with new teachers but it even occurs at times with veteran teachers. An effective principal will put in place processes to ensure that all teachers know the state standards specified for their subjects and grade level. The result of implementing and monitoring this fundamental requirement to know and teach to the standards will be that teachers teach the essential skills required by the state education department.

The same principle applies to any locally developed curricula. If the school district requires that certain standards or skills be taught, then it is a fundamental expectation and requirement that teachers teach them. This seems like another obvious point and it is. But, to the extent that teachers are teaching something other than the required standards, students are not learning what the state or district requires.

Such learning may be terrific for students. But it should be *purposefully planned* as an addition to the required curriculum *rather than in place of* the required curriculum. Again, it is the principal's responsibility to ensure that all teachers know and teach the required curricula and that any deviations from it are as a result of planned benefits for students, not because of teachers' ignorance of required standards or willful deviation from them.

3. *Conduct curriculum audits.* One effective way of ensuring that all standards are taught is to conduct a curriculum audit. An audit is an official examination or inspection which examines what is taught and what is not taught in the school. In a curriculum audit, the principal examines those factors or conditions that enable teachers to effectively teach the required curricula, or that hinder them from doing so.

Conducting a curriculum audit is a time-intensive process that requires the principal to be an instructional leader. You likely have heard the old saying, "If you do what you have always done, you'll get what you have always got." It doesn't take long for an observant principal to see which classrooms, subjects, or entire grades are producing inadequate results. Unless there is some change in the instruction occurring in those classrooms, subjects, or grades, it is reasonable to expect that the same inferior results will continue.

Data tells a story. It can be used to identify the classrooms, subjects, or entire grades most in need of improvement. Start doing a curriculum audit with those most needy classrooms, subjects, or grades. Share that data with the affected teachers and continually emphasize that you are working with them to improve outcomes of instruction.

Sometimes teachers feel like they are the targets of "data-shaming." That is, they feel like data is used to embarrass them or point out their deficient results. It is critical that teachers perceive that principals are doing something *for* them or *with* them rather than *to* them. Principals must be perceived as trustworthy and genuine in their efforts to improve instruction rather than as simply attempting to place blame.

Before undertaking a curriculum audit, build trust by building relationships, providing constructive feedback after observations of teachers, and involving teachers in analysis of student achievement data. When enlisting teachers as partners in the work of examining data as a tool to improve instruction, be careful to do so without making them feel belittled or inferior. At the same time, make it clear that no excuses will be accepted for inadequate results or instruction. A mantra that could be used as a philosophical basis for the work involved in curriculum audits is "No blame, no shame, and no excuses." Work diligently in collaboration with the affected teachers to examine these components of a curriculum audit:

- Is there a clear curriculum map that specifies what all teachers are responsible for teaching?
- Is there a list of all required performance indicators required to be taught in all subjects, such as K–6 reading?
- Are all of the performance indicators taught or are some of them not taught?
- Are there gaps in some standards being taught because teachers think different teachers are teaching them?
- Is the curriculum material "teacher friendly"?
- Is the curriculum document being used? If not, explore the reasons why.
- Is instruction sufficiently supported with textbook teachers' guides and other supplementary resources (such as technology, workbooks, DVDs, manipulatives, etc.)
- Are those resources readily available?
- Obtain a copy of several assessments used by teachers of the grade or curriculum area. Are assessments aligned with standards on which the curriculum is based?
- Is there evidence that the content, format, and rigor of the assessments are aligned with high-stakes assessments such as district end-of-unit tests, state tests, Advanced Placement exams, etc.?
- What suggestions do the teachers have for the improvement of the curriculum material?

- What suggestions do the teachers have for improving instruction in their subjects?

Answering these questions will give principals an audit or assessment of the instruction that is taking place. Principals and teachers can then decide upon the steps the school could take to improve student outcomes by increasing the alignment among the written, supported, taught, and assessed curricula.

4. *Thoroughly examine the results of core, daily instruction and do a causal analysis of problems.* All too often, when students are not performing well in a subject, the automatic reaction is to increase the amount of remediation offered to students. Albert Einstein (*New York Times*, May 25, 1946) said. "A new type of thinking is essential if mankind is to survive and move forward toward higher levels." Surely, some students need extra help to learn course content. However, before looking at extra help for students as an immediate and unequivocal solution, it is prudent to think in a new way.

Examine the regular, daily, Tier 1 instruction being provided to students. Is it effective? Is it effective in every teacher's classroom? How do you know? Is the inadequacy of core, daily instruction in some classrooms a contributing cause for the need for remediation? Could core, daily instruction be improved so that more students master essential content and fewer need remediation? Like many aspects of school issues, it is prudent to assess underlying causes of a problem before thinking that the most apparent or convenient solution to the issue is the most judicious one.

A useful strategy to examine the impact of core, daily instruction is a causal systems analysis or fishbone diagram. Often called a cause-and-effect diagram, this process helps educators move beyond superficial analyses to examine the underlying reasons for a problem and then to develop an improvement plan based upon that accurate analysis. Determining root causes of or underlying reasons for problems, such as the need for remedial instruction, is a precursor to creating effective action plans to solve those problems.

Remediation should be reserved only for those students who truly need it. It should not be a Band-Aid to cover up the consequences of insufficient core, daily instruction. Principals should resist the temptation to go for the obvious and easy "solution" of increasing remedial services to students who are not achieving well. Before jumping to that solution, take the time to do a root-cause analysis by examining the impact of core, daily instruction on student achievement.

Maybe core, daily instruction in your school truly prevents all but a few students from needing remediation. Or maybe it results in more students than necessary being referred to remediation. The only way to determine that is to do a causal-systems or root-cause analysis of the reasons students are placed in remedial classes or are not achieving to desired and expected levels.

It is important to realize that such a causal-systems analysis can also be used to address many other school problems. For example, what are the root causes for students having poor attendance, arriving late to classes, skipping classes, not doing homework, misbehaving in some classes but not others, etc. All of those issues impact the academic achievement of students. Although they may not be directly related to instruction, if a principal can improve upon these issues, then instruction and students' skills can be enhanced. A problem cannot be solved until its root causes are accurately and thoroughly, not superficially, identified. Once they have been identified, then solutions to address those causes can also be identified.

5. *Put the right teachers in the right assignments.* Much like a coach of a sports team puts some players in positions to maximize their strengths and some in positions to minimize their weaknesses, a principal must do the same with teachers. Not all teachers are masters of all subjects within their certification area. For example, at the elementary level, some teachers have a lot of passion for and expertise in teaching science. Others teach it because it is required, even though they do not have enthusiasm for it or are underprepared to do so.

At the secondary level, some teachers have more expertise at teaching geometry than calculus or U.S. history than European history. Of course, principals should continually work on building the capacity of their teachers and teaching assignments can change over time as teachers' skills broaden. But students only get one shot at each grade or subject. It is the principal's responsibility to put the most talented teachers available in front of students.

Being appropriately certified does not necessarily equate with being knowledgeable or talented enough to teach every subject within the certification area. Wise principals examine teachers' transcripts and talk with teachers about their strengths and areas for growth before making teaching assignments. Then, they assign teachers to grades or subjects where their skills will be maximized and their weaknesses minimized.

6. *Involve teachers in crafting solutions to instructional problems.* "A man convinced against his will is of the same opinion still." That quote, often attributed to Dale Carnegie in his 1936 book, *How to Win Friends and Influence People* (Carnegie 1936, 145), still rings true today. Principals are typically smart, conscientious people eager to solve and prevent problems to strengthen their schools. Sometimes in their eagerness to solve a problem, implement a new program, or improve instruction, they rush off in a

direction that may not be effective or they may not have the support of the people who will be required to implement it.

Typically, people closest to the issue know strategies for solving and preventing problems. To gain the benefit from involving people affected by decisions in crafting those decisions, a wise principal will form a "Principal's Advisory Committee," a "Curriculum Leadership Team," or a "Council for Excellence." The name of the group is somewhat important because it signifies the group's responsibility, but it is not the most important part of it. What is most important is that representative teachers have input into decisions that affect them and the school.

There are at least two benefits from forming such a leadership team. First, the principal will make better decisions because of the advice offered by teachers in the trenches, whose actions and support will be critical to successful implementation of initiatives. As teachers discuss the ramifications of proposed plans of action to improve instruction (or many other issues relevant to the school), they will consider impediments to the idea as well as actions to improve upon the principal's initial plans.

Through that refining process, a second major benefit will occur. Because representative teachers scrutinize ideas to improve instruction, they are much more likely to support the decisions made and be ambassadors for the plan among their colleagues. Thus, they will not have to implement something against their will while they have the same opinion still. Instead, the process of letting a school leadership team share in the crafting of important instructional decisions results in people who are convinced of the merits, because of their insightful collaboration, and ready to implement the plan because they support the agreed-upon action.

Does a principal abdicate responsibility by sharing decision making on instructional or other issues? No. Principals are charged with the responsibility for making decisions for maximum achievement of students as well as satisfaction with the school and that responsibility cannot be given away. The buck stops with the principal. Before forming a Principal's Advisory Committee, Curriculum Leadership Team, a Council for Excellence, or any similar group, the principal should make it clear that decisions made by such a committee are all *advisory* because the principal has the final responsibility and authority to make decisions.

There may be times when the principal does not agree with the committee's decisions and chooses to make decisions against its recommendations. More often than not, that will not be the case because reasonable, conscientious, representative teachers will typically make prudent decisions about instructional issues which the principal is likely to support. A principal's decisions are still likely to be supported even if the committee's advice is not followed, as long as it is clear that the rationales for its recommendations are understood and an explanation for the principal's alternative decision is communicated.

7. *Form Professional Learning Communities.* Edglossary.org defines a "Professional Learning Community" as follows:

> A *professional learning community*, or *PLC*, is a group of educators that meets regularly, shares expertise, and works collaboratively to improve teaching skills and the academic performance of students. The term is also applied to schools or teaching faculties that use small-group collaboration as a form of professional development . . . These three words explain the concept: Professionals coming together in a group—a community—to learn.

That is a very accurate description. As teachers come together to analyze data regarding test results, they will find that some teachers produced better results than others on individual test questions. Following that analysis should be a discussion of teaching strategies. "How did you teach that concept to get the results you got?" As a result of such frank discussions, teachers will learn effective strategies from fellow teachers.

The aforementioned refrain of "No blame, No Shame, No excuses" should form a philosophical basis for the actions of PLCs. No blame—teachers should not be maligned for producing inadequate results. Assume that each teacher acted conscientiously to effectively teach skills. No shame—no one should be made to feel guilty about test scores. No excuses—inadequate results are not an option. We are going to work together to find or develop effective teaching strategies to maximize the skills of our students. Test results will be a natural consequence of our highly effective teaching.

Three caveats are important for principals with regard to PLCs. The first is that the term Professional Learning Communities means different things to different people. It is essential for principals to meet with teachers to form a working definition of PLCs similar to the one cited above by edglossary. org. All teachers and the principal should have a common understanding that PLCs should analyze test data, share successful teaching practices, and give all team members an equal voice in respectfully sharing instructional concerns and offering solutions.

Such a common understanding of the intent of teachers working collaboratively together to improve results is critical, but the name "Professional Learning Communities" is not. If the term "Professional Learning Communities" has a negative connotation in your school or district, then change it to something more positive. Some ideas are Collaborative Learning Teams,

Data Teams, or Instructional Leadership Teams. Naming the team is an example of point 6 above: Involve teachers in crafting solutions to instructional problems.

Be pragmatic. There is no harm in letting teachers decide upon the name of the group as long as the essential function of it occurs. What is critical is that teachers work collaboratively together to analyze data and share successful teaching practices so that their skills and students' skills will increase. Regardless of what you call the team, many effective strategies for the functioning of those teams can be found with a quick search of the internet.

Next, principals should create a schedule that affords times for PLCs to meet. That can be done fairly easily at the elementary level by scheduling common times for art, music, physical education, and other special classes to meet by grade level. Doing so will allow, for example, third grade teachers to meet regularly while their classes are attending a special class.

At the middle school and high school levels, teachers of common subjects should be scheduled for planning periods at a common time, to the extent practical. Even though teachers may teach different grade levels, teachers of English, math, and history can offer their expertise to other teachers in the same subject area. That is also somewhat true of science teachers even though they may teach different science classes Therefore, scheduling those teachers to meet at consistent times can raise all of their skills.

Creating a schedule for teachers of a subject across grade levels can be challenging and will take creativity, persistence, and out-of-the-norm thinking. But the time spent developing such a schedule will pay dividends as teachers with common subject knowledge collaborate to strengthen their instruction.

The final point about PLCs relates to how a principal devotes their time. How one spends time is a clear indicator of what one values. Peruse the previous chapter entitled, "Management precedes leadership: Make the ordinary things ordinary" again. If the ordinary management functions of the school are, in fact, ordinary, then the principal has time to devote to higher-order, instructional leadership activities such as those being involved in Professional Learning Communities.

PLCs need effective leadership to ensure that the focus is on data analysis and examining teaching practices, rather than digressing into unrelated issues, and that all opinions are heard, not just those of people who are most inclined to talk. As time-consuming as it may be, if principals lead PLC meetings until they are confident that the PLC meetings can function effectively in their absence, then committing that time clearly indicates the value the principal holds for the potential of PLCs to increase teachers' skills and the academic performance of students.

If a school is too large for the principal to devote their own time to attending PLC meetings, then another tactic could be for the principal to train department heads, instructional coaches, lead teachers, or other similar personnel about how PLCs should effectively operate and have people in those positions lead those meetings.

8. *Tap the expertise of teachers to increase other teachers' skills.* You no doubt have heard the expression, "random acts of kindness." A variation of that term, which accurately describes what often happens in schools, is "random acts of progress."

Remember the key finding from the McKinsey organization, "A school's results can never exceed the quality of its teachers" (Barber and Mourshed 2007, 16). That premise compels principals to (1) continually develop the skills of their teachers and (2) work to make highly effective teaching practices consistent throughout the school, rather than having skillful teachers who teach effectively be "random acts of progress." Here are some actions principals might take to help teachers become more effective than the sum of their individual talents would otherwise permit.

Require new teachers to observe the classes of successful teachers to learn classroom management, lesson-planning, and instructional strategies. Similarly, ask veteran teachers to observe inexperienced teachers and provide them feedback to improve their skills.

Devote the time necessary to collaborate with teachers to devise an effective mentoring curriculum that requires the mentor to observe new teachers and provide constructive feedback to improve teaching skills. Then, assign highly effective mentors to new teachers throughout their entire probationary period. Mentors should do everything possible to help new teachers be successful—from helping with lesson planning and offering strategies for managing student behavior to navigating the political waters. In establishing the criteria for mentors, be sure to include a very positive attitude about teaching in addition to a strong record of successful teaching.

Make a bank of successful, proven lesson plans. Such lessons could be decided upon in Professional Learning Community meetings or by the principal's Instructional Leadership Team. That resource will increase the percentage of effective lessons delivered to students.

Every school has some outstanding teachers. Some may be exceptional because they have refined their craft over many years. Others may be National Board Certified Teachers or incorporate technology into their lessons in very effective ways. Regardless of how long they have been teaching or how they become excellent, astute principals can take advantage of such in-house resources by having them teach model lessons for their peers.

Principals can also help better future teachers by involving teachers in choosing which teachers to serve as sponsors for student teachers. It is essential that student teachers be assigned to practicing teachers who are excellent roles models—teachers whose teaching skills, work ethic, and attitude toward the profession and school are all worthy of emulation. More such strategies are explained in the chapter, "Creating conditions for success and retention of teachers."

9. *Structure Meaningful Professional Development.* Unfortunately, many teachers consider professional development activities to be a waste of time. Why? It could be that well-intentioned principals planned professional development activities that they thought would be useful for teachers without sufficiently seeking the input of teachers beforehand. A wise principal will collaborate with teachers to develop *teacher- directed professional development.*

There are many, many resources to plan professional development. The Association for Supervision and Curriculum Development (ASCD) has an abundance of resources to help teachers teach better. One such resource is Professional Development Online (PD Online) which contains a wealth of general and subject-specific videos and courses to help teachers increase their skills. Those practical, self-paced courses offered online are excellent resources to help teachers strengthen their teaching skills. Another simple but effective PD activity could be to send teachers to observe teachers at neighboring schools who are producing outstanding results so they can learn highly effective methods that could be replicated in their instructional practices.

In virtually every subject, there is a professional organization that teachers can use to increase teaching skills. The National Council of Teachers of Mathematics, the International Literacy Association, the National Science Teaching Association, and the National Council for the Social Studies have an abundance of resources for teachers of core subjects.

The Society of Health and Physical Educators, the Association for Middle Level Education, the International Society for Technology in Education, the Association for Computer Using Educators, the Association for the Advancement of Computing in Education, the American Association of School Librarians, the Association for Childhood Education International, the American Council on the Teaching of Foreign Languages, and the National Association for Gifted Children, etc., offer a plethora of resources to enhance teaching based upon best practices and research.

Remember the key point of planning *teacher-directed professional development*. To develop highly effective professional development, principals should work in partnership with their Principal's Advisory Committee, Curriculum Leadership Team, or Council for Excellence to craft meaningful, effective, productive professional development activities.

10. *How good can we be? Fostering continuous improvement.* All of the aforementioned actions should result in teachers continually improving their skills, which should result in increased academic performance for students. As significant improvement in the academic skills of students occurs, there could be a tendency for teachers and principals to rest on their collective laurels.

Highly effective principals commend and celebrate increased student achievement. But they don't stop there. Instead, they nurture a culture of excellence by asking questions such as: "How good can we be? What actions could we take to make substantial improvement? What would it take to have the best math scores in the district? How could we get the best reading scores in the region? What can we do next to better serve our students, school, and community? Are we serving the needs of ALL students in the school?" Those questions demonstrate a continual striving for excellence and result in continuous improvement. The principal is the chief driver of that culture of excellence.

None of the ten actions cited above are likely to happen organically. They all will require purposeful, intentional, continual leadership by the principal if they are to occur and be successful. The job as a principal is sometimes described as the hardest job you will ever love. That is an apt description. Being a principal is hard work and immensely satisfying. To continually raise the skill and effectiveness of teachers requires principals to be persistent in their instructional leadership actions. Perhaps this quote by former president Calvin Coolidge will serve as motivation for this important work:

> Nothing in this world can take the place of persistence. Talent will not; nothing is more common than unsuccessful men with talent. Genius will not; unrewarded genius is almost a proverb. Education will not; the world is full of educated derelicts. Persistence and determination alone are omnipotent. The slogan Press On! has solved and always will solve the problems of the human race.
>
> —Calvin Coolidge[2]

Leading instructional improvement takes hard work and persistence to bring about excellent results. Press on.

Questions to Consider

1. Do teachers in my school teach from bell-to-bell?
2. Do teachers in my school review objectives for each lesson and check for understanding throughout it and at the end of lessons?
3. Do teachers in my school proactively develop relationships with students?
4. How often do students in my school straggle into class after the bell rings? Why?
5. What are some ways that teachers and principals could encourage students to get to class on time?
6. Do teachers see problems as the responsibility of administrators to solve rather than seeing themselves as part of the problem-solving and instructional-improvement process?
7. Have I, as the principal, worked with teachers to determine the underlying causes of problems, not just the presenting symptoms of a problem?
8. Have I, as the principal, created a culture and structure where everyone in the school feels like it is part of their job to solve problems rather than viewing them as only the administrator's responsibility?
9. Does my school have a plan to ensure that all teachers know the state and local standards they are responsible for teaching?
10. Do teachers have a readily available list of the standards to be taught, as well as scope and sequence documents and/or pacing charts for the subject and grade level?
11. Does my school have a plan or process to ensure that teachers actually teach those standards?
12. If teachers teach something other than the required state or local standards, have such units been approved?
13. What evidence is there to verify that core, daily instruction is effective rather than a contributing cause to the need for remediation?
14. Are teachers in my school placed in assignments to maximize their strengths?
15. Does my school have committees such as a Principal's Advisory Committee, Curriculum Leadership Team, or Council for Excellence to craft solutions to educational issues?
16. Does my school have highly functioning Professional Learning Communities? If not, what actions could we take to implement them?
17. Are there ongoing practices in place to allow teachers to tap the expertise of teachers to increase their skills?

18. Is there ongoing collaboration with teachers to structure productive professional development activities? Are teachers aware of the abundance of resources available to them from their professional organizations?
19. Is there a culture of excellence in the school? Do the administrators and teachers ask "How good can we be?" and develop actions for continuous improvement?

References

ASCD. (2020). http://www.ascd.org/Default.aspx.

Barber, M., and Mourshed, M. (2007). *How the world's best-performing school systems come out on top.* London: McKinsey.

Dean, C., Hubbell, E., Pitler, H., and Stone, B. (2012). *Classroom instruction that works: Research-based strategies for increasing student achievement,* second edition. Alexandria, VA: ASCD/Denver, CO: McREL.

Carnegie, D. (1936). *How to win friends and influence people.* New York: Simon & Schuster.

Einstein, A. (1946, May 25). Atomic education urged by Einstein: Scientist in plea for $200,000 to promote new type of essential thinking. *New York Times.* Retrieved from https://www.nytimes.com/1946/05/25/archives/atomic-education-urged-by-einstein-scientist-in-plea-for-200000-to.html.

Great Schools Partnership. (2014, March 3). Professional learning community. *Glossary of Education Reform.* Retrieved from https://www.edglossary.org/professional-learning-community/.

Solution Tree. (2020). All things PLC, all in one place. AllThingsPLC. Retrieved from https://www.allthingsplc.info/.

~

CHAPTER FOUR

A Three-Step Process for Improving Virtually Any Aspect of a School

Overcoming the Seven Steps of Stagnation with the Success Questions

> Around here we don't look backwards for very long. We keep moving forward, opening up new doors and doing new things, because we're curious . . . and curiosity keeps leading us down new paths. (Walt Disney)[1]

Continually improving one's school is an inherent responsibility of being a principal and provides a great degree of satisfaction for principals. The status quo typically is not an option. Test scores need to be improved. Some groups of students are meeting or exceeding standards, others are not. Attendance overall may be good but some students are chronically absent. Most teachers are highly skilled, but there are some on the left side of the bell curve whose performance needs to improve, etc. A principal's list of things to improve upon is usually lengthy.

Despite the need for improvement in many areas of the school, principals' efforts to improve the school are often hindered by resisters. Their sense of inertia or outright opposition can broadly be characterized as the seven steps of stagnation. This chapter will provide principals with a practical, three-step process to improve the outcomes of schools and overcome the seven steps of stagnation by turning resisters into supporters.

A Three-Step Process for Improving Virtually Any Aspect of a School
How does a principal go about improving the many and varied functions of a school? Here is a simple and effective three-step process:

1. Analyze the status of your school with regard to whatever issue needs to be improved, for example, test scores, attendance rates, graduation rates, reducing disciplinary referrals, strengthening curricula.
2. Find a standard of excellence regarding the issue to be improved.
3. Implement an action plan to move the school from its current status to achieve the standard of excellence.

The first step in this three-step improvement process is to "*Analyze the status of your school.*" In his best-selling book entitled, *Good to Great,* author Jim Collins coined the apt expression, "Confront the Brutal Facts" (Collins 2001, 65). In essence, that means look closely at the data, even if it is negative; especially if it is negative. Your school is what it is. Data is impartial and tells a story. Don't try to sugarcoat lousy or inadequate results. The results are what they are. When examining test scores, discipline referrals, attendance rates, culture, and other indicators of school quality there are likely many areas in need of improvement.

The second step in the three-step improvement process is to "*Find a standard of excellence regarding the issue to be improved.*" A logical starting point to find standards of excellence could be determining what is prescribed by the school district or state department of education regarding the issue in need of improvement. A strategy to do so could be a simple internet search for "standards of quality for" or "standards of excellence for."

But, beyond those good starting points, principals can access the wisdom of numerous professional organizations that have thoroughly researched their fields and determined high-quality standards. Some organizations that have published quality standards in the most common areas where principals would want to lead school improvement efforts are: the International Literacy Association, the National Council of Teachers of Mathematics, the American Historical Association, the National Science Teaching Association, the National Association of Special Education Teachers, and the Teaching Institute for Excellence in STEM.

Other national organizations have established high-quality standards for noncore subjects, including the International Society for Technology in Education, the American Council on the Teaching of Foreign Languages, the Society of Health and Physical Educators, the National Art Education Association, the Music Teachers National Association, the American Association of School Librarians, the School Social Work Association of America, and the American School Counselor Association. These subject-specific, national organizations can provide principals with in-depth knowledge and resources to facilitate school improvement initiatives.

In addition, there are national organizations that promulgate standards of excellence for students' health, safety, and vitality. Some notable ones include the Substance Abuse and Mental Health Services Administration and the U.S. Department of Health and Humans Services which offers sage advice about preventing teenage pregnancy and stopping bullying. Attendance Works has an abundance of resources to help principals improve the attendance of students.

Principals could also examine the quality standards championed by the National School Safety Center, the National School Climate Center, the Community Anti-Drug Coalitions of America, and the National Student Council's National Council of Excellence recognition awards.

There are also national organizations that offer resources specific to the grade range of schools. Principals can find an abundance of resources from the National Association of Elementary School Principals, the Association for Middle Level Education, and the National Association of Secondary School Principals. Furthermore, the American Association of School Administrators and the Association for Supervision and Curriculum Development offer excellent resources for principals at any level.

As one can see, there are numerous national organizations whose mission is to foster excellence regarding many issues faced by school principals. Those organizations offer varying degrees of specificity about standards of quality. With some time spent researching them, a determined principal can garner many excellent principles and practices to determine high-quality standards—the second step in the three-step improvement process. Some examples are provided below that will illustrate how this second step in the three-step improvement process, *"Find a standard of excellence regarding the issue to be improved"* could work.

Most people would agree that the ability to understand and be able to apply mathematical knowledge well is a foundational, essential, skill for success in school and life. Suppose the data shows that the school is achieving weak, inadequate results in math. An excellent source of standards and successful practices regarding math instruction is the National Council of Teachers of Mathematics (nctm.org). By perusing that website, a principal could find a wealth of information about components of effective math programs and recommended teaching practices.

For example the NCTM's publications "Focus in High School Mathematics: Reasoning and Sense Making" and "Principles and Standards for School Mathematics" cite a number of successful practices regarding linking research and practice such as Reasoning with Numbers and Measurements, Reasoning with Algebraic Symbols, Reasoning with Functions, Reasoning with

Geometry, and Reasoning with Statistics and Probability. Further scrutiny of that website and its related resources can equip principals with knowledge to bridge the gap between current results and excellent results.

Another example of an area needing improvement is attendance. Many schools could improve the skills of students by improving their attendance, particularly those students who are chronically absent. Attendance Works (attendanceworks.org) cites the importance of attendance and offers a multitude of resources to help principals improve attendance including a "Toolkit for Principals" to lead attendance improvement initiatives. It also provides resources principals could use to involve families and community organizations in actions to increase attendance.

The brutal facts have been confronted. You have determined where you are. And you don't like it. There is a gap between the present status of your school with regard to . . . and the standard of excellence described by the aforementioned organizations. As the principal, the leader of the school, you know the problem and pertinent resources to help solve it. You are now ready to take the most critical step in the three-step improvement process: *"Implement an action plan to move the school from its current status to achieve the standard of excellence."*

Like teachers, principals are empathetic to the needs of students and are committed to helping them. They are also smart, talented people of action. Because of their dedication to helping students and their eagerness to do so, they might be inclined to develop action plans and get going on solving the immediate problem without fully involving people who would be affected by the action plan in the process of developing it. That would be a mistake. As mentioned in the previous chapters, process matters.

What is the difference between a marching band director and a man out for a walk? A marching band director has people following him because he is only a few steps ahead of the band members. If he gets too far ahead of his band, say a block or two, he is just a man out for a walk because no one is following him. Similarly, a principal must have followers. Otherwise, he is just a man out for a walk, a lone ranger.

So, principals are wise to temper their enthusiasm to quickly and independently solve problems and think through a process to initiate change that will involve people in crafting viable solutions which they will support because of their involvement. A good place to start is by generating discontent with the status quo. Data helps to create such dissatisfaction with the current status of X and subsequent desire to improve results. Showing people data regarding the brutal facts of the situation will typically make the need for change quite apparent.

Another effective strategy is to discuss the moral imperative for the change. Talking through questions like the following help to compel people to want to improve X. "What will be the consequence if we maintain the status quo rather than improving?" "What will be the impact on the students, the school, and the community?"

"How can we help students to achieve more?" "How can we raise our expectations for students and ourselves?" "How can we best serve our students, our school, and our community?" "Will students be well-prepared to be successful in careers or college with the skills we are providing for them?" "Instead of having these weak results, what would it take for us to have excellent results?"

After people have seen compelling data necessitating the change and have resolved that they can and must do better, the process of planning effective strategies can begin. The National Association of Secondary School Principals has identified a proven process/model for principals to consider using when leading change. The "Six-Step Process Circle for Initiative/Program Planning" includes these key steps in planning for a successful initiative:

1. Gather and analyze data to determine priorities
2. Explore possible solutions
3. Assess readiness and build capacity
4. Create and communicate the improvement plan
5. Implement the plan
6. Monitor and adjust

Those steps should be undertaken deliberately and in collaboration with affected stakeholders rather than done "lone ranger" style. Be a marching band director rather than just a man out for a walk. By following the steps to (1) *analyze the status of your school*, (2) *find a standard of excellence regarding the issue to be improved*, and (3) *implement an action plan to move the school from its current status to achieve the standard of excellence*, principals will greatly improve outcomes for students and experience much satisfaction in the process.

The result will be beautiful music—greatly improved results for students and the principal. Much more information on implementing school improvement initiatives is in the chapter entitled "Crafting a school improvement plan."

Overcoming the Seven Steps of Stagnation with the Success Questions

Despite the importance of continual improvement, resulting in better opportunities for students, principals' efforts to improve aspects of the school are often met with resistance from teachers, staff, and sometimes parents. Every school likely has some "CAVE" people. CAVE is an acronym for Citizens Against Virtually Everything. They are the resisters, blockers, and negative people whose automatic inclination when an idea is presented is to think about reasons why something can't be done rather than thinking about ways to improve the organization. No matter how good an idea may be, how many people are for it, or how much it will help students or improve the school, they are against it.

Erwin M. Soukup is credited with coining "The Seven Steps to Stagnation." They are:

1. We've never done it that way before.
2. We're not ready for that.
3. We are doing all right without trying that.
4. We tried it once before.
5. We don't have money for that.
6. That's not our job.
7. Something like that can't work.

Chances are that those statements probably sound familiar to you. That is because, in virtually every school in the nation, a cadre of CAVE people have expressed some version of the seven steps of stagnation. What must a principal do to implement needed change when met by CAVE people entrenched in this way? Whenever a principal contemplates implementing a plan or initiative, they should anticipate that some version of the seven steps of stagnation will be stated. A wise, forward-thinking principal should be prepared to provide cogent responses to each type of these negative responses.

In addition, principals should anticipate the possibility that staff members may attempt to thwart implementation of an initiative by doing an "end-run" to the superintendent or to parents. By spreading misinformation, detractors intend to get momentum going against the initiative.

Principals can prevent the success of those end-runs by continually keeping the superintendent informed of the status of initiatives, meeting regularly with parent groups such as the PTA or PTO, and providing regular updates on improvement initiatives on the school's webpage or via other communication vehicles. A question-and-answer format which addresses specific issues can be a helpful tool to provide accurate information. See more strategies to gain support for initiatives in the chapter entitled, "Communicating to build confidence in you and your school."

Next, the principal can turn the tables on CAVE people and make a case for needed change by asking the "Success Questions." The Success Questions cause CAVE people and others to realize that positive change is needed. They are:

1. Is what we are now doing with regard to _____ getting us what we want?
2. What do we really want with regard to _____? What is our vision?
3. What experiences, knowledge, or research will help us achieve our wants?
4. How does our new knowledge influence our present beliefs with regard to_____?
5. Which of our present practices will help us achieve our wants?
6. What ineffective actions can we stop and replace with actions that will help us to achieve our goals?
7. Which present practices need to be changed so that they align to our wants, what we know, and what we believe?
8. What actions should we take as a result of this analysis?

Principals are change agents. Change agents will typically have to overcome CAVE people who want to stymie progress by dwelling on the seven steps of stagnation. By thinking deeply about answers to the seven steps of stagnation and proactively engaging people in the Success Questions, principals can stimulate and sustain positive change.

The next chapter will show a very practical application of this three-step plan for improving any aspect of a school and overcoming the seven steps of stagnation as it leads the reader through the essential skills of "Crafting a school improvement plan."

Questions to Consider

1. Does data about my school indicate areas in need of significant improvement?
2. Have I involved significant stakeholders in analyzing that data so they see the same problems I do?
3. What organizations have established high-quality standards and practices that could help guide the improvement process?
4. Has the need for change been broadly and effectively communicated?
5. Have I helped to generate discontent with the status quo?

6. What planning process will lead to improved results?
7. Who should be involved in improvement initiatives? Why? What will their role be?
8. Am I acting as a marching band director or just a person out for a walk?

1. As I consider improvement plans, have I also developed convincing answers to the "Seven Steps of Stagnation?"
2. What actions may need to be taken as a result of answers to the Success Questions?

References

American Association of School Administrators (AASA). https://education.state university.com/pages/1755/American-Association-School-Administrators.html.

American Association of School Librarians (AASL). https://www.google.com/search ?q=American+Association+of+School+Librarians&oq=American+Association +of+School+Librarians&aqs=chrome..69i57.1030j0j1&sourceid=chrome&ie= UTF-8

American Council on the Teaching of Foreign Languages (ACTFL). https://www .actfl.org/.

American Historical Association. https://www.historians.org/about-aha-and -membership/affiliated-societies/organization-of-history-teachers.

American School Counselor Association. https://www.schoolcounselor.org/.

Association for Middle Level Education (AMLE). https://www.amle.org/.

Association for Supervision and Curriculum Development (ASCD). http://www .ascd.org/Default.aspx.

Attendance Works. https://www.attendanceworks.org/.

Collins, J. (2001). *Good to great: Why some companies make the leap . . . and others don't.* New York: HarperCollins.

Community Anti-Drug Coalitions of America (CADCA). https://www.cadca.org/.

International Literacy Association. https://literacyworldwide.org/get-resources/ standards.

International Society for Technology in Education. https://www.iste.org/.

Music Teachers National Association. https://www.mtna.org/.

National Art Education Association. https://www.arteducators.org/.

National Association of Elementary School Principals (NAESP). https://www.naesp .org/.

National Association of Secondary School Principals (NASSP). Six-step process circle for initiative/program planning. Retrieved from https://www.nassp.org/ professional-learning/online-professional-development/leading-success/discussion -guide-planning-templates/.

National Association of Special Education Teachers. https://www.naset.org/.

National Council of Teachers of Mathematics. https://www.nctm.org/.

National School Climate Center. https://www.schoolclimate.org/.

National School Safety Center. http://www.schoolsafety.us/.

National Science Teaching Association. https://www.nsta.org/.

National Student Council (NatStuCo). Council recognition: National council of excellence. https://www.natstuco.org/council-recognition/national-councils-of-excellence/.

School Social Work Association of America. https://www.sswaa.org/.

Society of Health and Physical Educators. https://www.shapeamerica.org/.

Substance Abuse and Mental Health Services Administration. Center for Substance Abuse Prevention. https://www.samhsa.gov/about-us/who-we-are/offices-centers/csap.

Teaching Institute for Excellence in STEM (TIES). https://www.tiesteach.org/.

U.S. Department of Health and Human Services. Office of Population Affairs. Adolescent health. https://www.hhs.gov/ash/oah/adolescent-development/reproductive-health-and-teen-pregnancy/teen-pregnancy-and-childbearing/teen-pregnancy-prevention-program/index.html and https://www.stopbullying.gov/.

~

CHAPTER FIVE

Crafting a School Improvement Plan

Continuous Improvement Consists of Goal-Setting and Motivating Teams

We can, whenever and wherever we choose, successfully teach all children whose schooling is of interest to us. We already know more than we need in order to do this. Whether we do it must finally depend on how we feel about the fact that we haven't so far." (Dr. Ron Edmonds, A Blueprint for Action II)[1]

All schools are required to develop an annual school improvement plan under the federal Every Students Succeeds Act which was signed into law in December of 2015 (ESSA 2015). Making an annual school improvement plan is an excellent way to improve a school because it is much like a roadmap that can lead to higher levels of student achievement and overall school improvement. It is a tangible means of implementing actions to achieve the vision of a school.

When thoughtfully developed with ample stakeholder participation and widespread dissemination of it, a school improvement plan can be a powerful driver of continuous growth. Furthermore, the process of continual improvement and awareness that one's school is committed to systematically getting better can be a source of pride for school personnel and the school-community, resulting in an ongoing desire to keep on improving.

Here are a dozen salient questions to consider when formulating a school improvement plan:

1. What data must be examined to identify improvement priorities?
2. What caused the results that we currently have?

3. Which actions will have the greatest impact upon improving student achievement?
4. Who should be involved in crafting the plan?
5. Who should play key roles in the implementation of the school improvement plan?
6. Is staff development needed to facilitate implementation of the school improvement plan?
7. Who should be informed about the school improvement plan to gain support for it?
8. What resources are needed to implement the plan?
9. What timeline is best for implementation of the action plans?
10. How should the action plans be monitored?
11. What evidence will verify if the plan is, or is not, meeting the intended results?
12. What is the best way to structure the school improvement plan?

Principals and school leaders must think through these interrelated questions and many others to design and implement effective school improvement plans to meet the ESSA requirements and continually improve schools. The following elaboration on each of these questions can provide guidance to principals as they craft successful school improvement plans to put their schools on the path of continuous improvement.

1. *What data must be examined to identify improvement priorities?* There are likely many areas in need of improvement in most schools. Typical areas include: increasing English Language Arts and mathematics skills, improving attendance and the graduation rate, decreasing behavioral referrals, and improving results for minority, special education, and low-wealth students.

Step one in crafting a school improvement plan is to analyze trend data from pertinent assessments to identify deficient scores (as a result of deficient skills). Data tells a story. Look for patterns in data over several years indicating a consistent, pressing problem. What is the data revealing regarding overall passing and failure rates? Are there segments of the overall population that are not achieving as well as they could? Examine the failure and passing rates of all students on standardized assessments, including possible subgroups of students based on race, gender, income security, special education requirements, or other criteria. The data will tell a story about which groups are doing well and which are not.

It is certainly prudent to spend time, effort, and resources to bring all students to a level of proficiency, but that should not be the sole focus of principals. Schools educate all students, not only those who are struggling. It is incumbent upon principals and their schools to find ways to help all students become all that they are capable of becoming. As a result of that philosophy, it is also judicious for school leaders to work to raise the level of mastery for those students who have already reached proficiency.

2. *What caused the results that we currently have?* Once the "what" is determined, inadequate skills and tests scores, it is critical to determine the "why" that caused those results. This is an essentially important question. Without knowing why results occurred, a school improvement team could very well spend time and effort attempting to solve the wrong problem.

Let's take weak math results on a standardized assessment as an example of the need to do a causal analysis of the reasons for insufficient results. When analyzing objective test data, start with an item analysis, a record of how many students answered questions correctly and incorrectly. Suppose the results of the item analysis showed that a large percentage of students missed questions that tested concepts A, B, and C.

Why did they miss those questions? Did most students pick the same incorrect answer? How could the distinction between the correct answer and the incorrect answer be taught more effectively? Were the standards tested actually taught? Were they taught in the right sequence? Did students in some classes do well on those questions while students in other classes did not? Did some subgroups do well while others did not?

Did students not understand the processes necessary to solve the problems? Was their failure to solve the problem the result of not reading the problem correctly? Were students confused about different vocabulary being used on the state test compared to what teachers use in daily instruction? Did the students who scored poorly also have language or attendance issues? The answers to those and related questions help to identify the causes of insufficient results and serve as the basis for solving the right problems.

It would be a very effective use of a principal's time to lead such a comprehensive "root-cause" analysis before crafting an improvement plan. Creating a "fishbone diagram" is a tool to implement a causal analysis to determine the root cause of problems. The spines in the diagram of a fish represent possible causes of the problem. If principals are not already aware of how to create a "fishbone diagram" that identifies the root causes of problems, they can educate themselves by readily accessing videos and related explanations from scholarly websites or their professional organizations. Some pertinent sources of additional information are also listed in the references section for this chapter.

A very efficient process for conducting a causal analysis or root-cause analysis of a problem is the "Why-why-why" method stated in *Southeast*

Education Network magazine (April 2015). It states, "Define a student learning problem. Analyze at least three data sources to accurately pinpoint the problem."

1. Clearly state the student learning problem in writing. This formalizes and supports shared understanding of the issue.
2. Engage in collaborative dialogue with your team. Ask, "Why do we have this problem?" Then record the response beginning with "Because . . ."
3. Continue this process by repeating "step 2" three to five times until you feel a root cause has been identified.
4. Discuss the causes. Do any need confirmation? What other data can be consulted? Which one seems to be the root cause—the one that, if changed, will yield results? Now your team is ready to start generating solutions.

Much like the tip of an iceberg only identifies what is seen as opposed to what is underwater, a superficial analysis of the causes of a problem only identifies what is readily apparent. To implement fundamental, effective solutions to weak skills and weak test results, principals must identify the root causes of problems that may not be so easily seen. That takes much more work than jumping to conclusions or fixing what may be most easily fixed. Extensively examining fundamental problems and their root causes can result in the essential school improvement process of finding effective long-lasting solutions to them.

3. *Which actions will have the greatest impact upon improving student achievement?* Having identified the "What"—inadequate skills manifested by inadequate test results, and the "Why"—the root causes of weak skills, principals can now consider which actions will have the greatest impact to address the factors causing the problems.

A loose metaphor to describe such purposeful actions is that of a road trip. Leading the attainment of high achievement by all students is not like a short trip to the neighborhood store. It is more like a "road trip." First, you have decide where you want to go. Let's say you want to drive from Seattle to Boston. Such a trip would cause you to identify issues that must be considered on the long trip you want to take—the cost of gas, tolls, and lodging; routes to minimize road construction; driver fatigue due to the sheer distance; mountain passes; etc.

Maybe you want to get there as fast as you can while spending the least amount of money. Or, maybe making the best time at the lowest cost is not as important as seeing Mt. Rushmore, the Rock and Roll Hall of Fame in Cleveland, and Niagara Falls along the way.

Having identified your destination and how you want to experience the trip, then you can plan the most efficient way to get there. There may, in fact, be several viable and attractive options. Just like the cost of tolls, gas, and lodging, and the inconvenience of road construction, there are obstacles that must be overcome along the road to high achievement. In addition to the root causes your team identified, a principal's journey to high achievement for all students may be hindered by a lack of resources, language barriers, transience, etc. That is the reality of the situation. It is what it is.

There is an old saying attributed to Henry Ford, "Obstacles are those frightful things you see when you take your eyes off your goal."[2] Before him, Confucius stated, "When it is obvious that the goals cannot be reached, don't adjust the goals, adjust the action steps."[3] Those quotes are both accurate and motivational for school leaders.

Your route or, specifically, your action plan will be the high-yield actions that you and your team identify to overcome the obstacles along the road to high achievement. Typical action plans might include strengthening core, daily instruction by more proactively teaching key concepts, grouping for more effective instruction, aligning assessments with standards, and even changing teaching assignments. All actions should be based upon mitigating the root causes of problems preventing high achievement. You will likely consider many actions and rule some out because they are not as high-yield as others. Keep those that most expeditiously get you where you want to go on your road trip to attaining high achievement by all students.

Each school's improvement plan should be aligned with district goals and support attainment of them. Plans are most effective and measurable when they are written as SMART goals: specific, measurable, attainable, relevant, and time-bound. The more precise the goals are in terms of a score or some other measure of quality, the clearer the target for the action teams and the better their attainment can be judged. Here are some examples of SMART goals:

- Increase the percentage of students scoring at level 4 on the end-of-course state English Language Arts exam by 5 percent in grade 3.
- Increase the percentage of students attaining mastery level on the end-of-course Integrated Algebra exam by 10 percent.
- Increase the percentage of students taking Advanced Placement exams by 5 percent effective with the next school year.

- By February 15, present a cost-effective plan to the Superintendent of Schools to implement pre-Kindergarten effective with the next school year.
- Increase the percentage of special education students scoring at level 3 on the grades 3–5 math exam by 5 percent.

4. *Who should be involved in crafting the plan?* Determining solutions to root-cause problems that result in weak skills and test scores is a prime example of an issue that principals should tackle in collaboration with their leadership team (Principal's Advisory Committee, Council for Excellence, or Instructional Leadership team, whatever it is named in various schools).

Teachers are essential players in the attainment of goals. Based upon a thorough causal or root-cause analysis, the principal can work in collaboration with insightful, representative teachers to identify and implement the most impactful high-yield actions necessary to solve the identified problems. Like many other issues tackled by such an advisory committee, the fruit of its labor is likely to result in better decisions with greater support.

As has been emphasized a number of times in this book, principals should involve people in issues that affect them such as these curriculum and instructional leadership issues. To create meaningful strategic priorities that teachers, parents, the PTA, and other community members will support, principals should also consider involving insightful people such as directors of curriculum and instruction, lead teachers, instructional coaches, and department heads contribute in a significant way. Like other shared decision-making issues, seeking out people who have expertise to offer and/or the respect of their peers will enhance the decision-making process and support of those decisions.

5. *Who should play key roles in the implementation of the school improvement plan?* Once the action plans have been determined, or at least tentatively planned, then critical decisions need to be made about who will be the key leader implementing those plans. No one ever erected a statue to a committee. If achieving a goal is the responsibility of a committee, then, really, no one single person is responsible for attainment of the action plan. Committee members could easily rationalize failure by claiming that some other committee member was supposed to do something but did not.

Without a doubt, the attainment of goals is done with the cooperation of many people. But someone has to say, "This is my responsibility. I own it. I am the orchestra director who will coordinate all of the moving pieces of this issue. I will see that the job gets done." That key person could be an assistant principal, a department head, or a talented teacher. The position

Table 5.1.   Examples of SMART Goals with Designation of a Lead Participant.

Goal	Level: Increase	Lead Participant	Deadline
Increase number of students attaining mastery level on end-of-course math exams	Grade 6: 3% Grade 7: 3% Grade 8: 5%	Middle School Principal	End of course
Increase number of students scoring at level 4 on end-of-course state English Language Arts exam	Grade 3: 5%	Elementary Principal	End of course
Increase number of students taking Advanced Placement exams effective in next school year	Grades 9–12: 5%	High School Principal	May 15

may not matter as much as the person's attitude. A can-do attitude, holding the respect of the people involved, and perseverance are critical attributes the lead person must possess.

Ideally such a person will volunteer to lead the way. If not, the principal will have to tap the person most likely to get the job done. A clear and effective final *goals document* could look something like this example below. The position of SMART goals within the school's *action plan* is shown at the end of this chapter.

6. *Is staff development needed to facilitate implementation of the school improvement plan?* Each school's professional development plan should be aligned with support of district goals. To implement most improvement plans, teachers and other key movers will likely already have the skills they need to implement action plans. But if specific skills are needed to achieve the improvement target goals, for example training to teach Advanced Placement courses or training on specific reading or math teaching strategies, then a principal will need to ensure that teachers get the training they need to successfully implement the school improvement plan.

7. *Who should be informed about the school improvement plan to gain support for it?* Certainly, those people involved in implementing the plan should be regularly reminded of their role in achieving it. At a minimum, every employee in the school should also be apprised of the school improvement plan and its various components. The support of most school employees will be beneficial in achieving the plan and people will not support a plan that they are unaware of or don't understand. Principals must, therefore, cause the plan to be clearly and comprehensively explained so that everyone in the school understands it. That should not be a one-time event. Rather, by keeping the

plan—and related responsibilities—at the forefront of people's minds, their focus on it will sharpen and, ideally, their commitment to achieving it will increase.

In addition, principals should always keep the superintendent of schools informed about important issues. The superintendent of schools, the assistant superintendent for curriculum and instruction, or some other pertinent supervisor(s) should be aware of the school improvement plan. People in those positions will quite likely be sources of knowledge and support. Principals should not be hesitant about enlisting their help as needed. Every superintendent wants every school in the district to be successful and will quite likely provide help as needed.

The external school-community should also be informed of the school improvement plan and there are at least two benefits to informing them. One is that the parents, business owners, community members, and other stakeholders realize that the school is not resting on its laurels. Rather, the school is pushing and challenging itself to continually improve. That realization results in respect for the school, the principal, and members of the school improvement team.

Secondly, awareness of the plan could result in help from community members. That help could be expertise from knowledgeable experts within the community, financial underwriting of necessary professional development or technology, or maybe the donation of pizza or ice cream for school improvement team meetings. When credibility for the school has been established by creating a school improvement plan and, in successive years, achieving that plan, then asking for resources from the community becomes easier.

But obtaining resources from the community is an ancillary benefit. The real benefit of making the community aware of the components of a school improvement plan is that doing so builds confidence in the school and credibility for the principal.

In sum, the goals of the school improvement plan should be widely disseminated—posted on the school's webpage and in the halls of the school, written about in school newsletters and other communications to parents, talked about in presentations at civic organizations, etc. In addition to gaining respect for the school, such widespread distribution of the plan also creates a bit of public accountability. If many, many people understand the school improvement plan, a greater expectation for achieving it will occur. In addition to the satisfaction and pride that comes with achieving a worthy goal, a bit of pressure to achieve is one more motivator.

Among the many roles principals play, being a cheerleader is one of them. Principals can inspire their action teams to persevere by reporting on positive results, giving them guidance on how to strengthen results, or encouraging them to overcome challenges. Where a principal spends their time is indicative of what they think is valuable. The principal should be the chief supporter and monitor of the school improvement plan.

8. *What resources are needed to implement the plan?* The school improvement team must have the necessary resources to succeed. Time may be the biggest resource needed. Principals will need to collaborate with teachers to find time before or after school or free up time during the school day to provide teachers with sufficient opportunities to craft strategies to achieve the plan, learn new skills if necessary, and also to monitor its progress.

One fairly cost-effective way that many schools have found effective to free teachers to work on a school improvement plan is to hire substitute teachers. The substitute teachers can sub for one group of teachers to give them a chance to work on some component of the school improvement plan in the morning. Then, in the afternoon, the same substitute teachers can sub for a different group of teachers to work on a different component of the school improvement plan. Having half a day to work on the school improvement plan enables teachers to have a period for sustained thought while also allowing them to not be away from their classrooms for very long.

Just like schools, the school district will seldom have enough money to meet all of its needs. But, school improvement is a top priority. If principals make their school improvement plan consistent with district priorities and keep key central office personnel informed, funds may be available from them to supplement the school's budget to achieve the school improvement plan.

9. *What is the timeline for implementation of the action plans?* Unless dates are set for attainment of goals, then plans are not actually plans, they are just aspirational statements or platitudes, something that hopefully will happen someday. Specificity about when actions will begin and end matters because setting dates for the implementation of actions causes teams to get their essential work done to hit those target dates. Knowing what needs to be accomplished and when it needs to be accomplished typically results in conscientious people doing the necessary work to hit the target.

Therefore, it is essential to state target dates for completion in the school improvement plan document. Target dates often coincide with end-of-course assessments, as in the examples in the table above. But they could also occur during the school year, for example:

Table 5.2. Example of a School Improvement Goal Due During the School Year.

Goal	Lead Participant	Deadline
Make cost-effective recommendations to Superintendent of Schools plans to implement Pre-Kindergarten effective next school year	Elementary School Principal	March 1

10. *How should the action plans be monitored?* A plan cannot simply be created and left alone. Monitoring the implementation and effectiveness of action plans is essential. To gauge the effectiveness of a plan, a principal must monitor whether it is implemented with fidelity by everyone involved. The action planning team must also establish reasonable indicators of quality or benchmarks along the way.

To use the road trip metaphor again, you know you're on the right road to Cleveland when you pass by Chicago. The school improvement plan should state what progress is expected to be seen as a result of implementation of the action plan and when that progress should be examined. For example, it might be reasonable to see incremental progress at the end of each five- or ten-week period.

Much like a coach of a sports team makes decisions as the season progresses and during in-game situations by continually monitoring and adjusting, establishing benchmarks and dates for the attainment of goals enables the team to gauge progress and take action to intervene along the way, if need be, to achieve their intended results. As the "quality-control" person for every aspect of the school, the principal should ensure that the school improvement plan progresses as intended and any necessary adjustments to it are made.

11. *What evidence will verify if the plan is, or is not, meeting the intended results?* Results matter. Ideally, if the principal and school improvement team have been monitoring and adjusting the plan throughout the school year, their refinement actions have resulted in achievement of the intended results. The advantage of setting SMART goals is that it makes judging the attainment of goals easy. If a specific goal was set, for example increasing the percentage of students attaining mastery on the third grade state reading exam by 5 percent by the end of the school year, then it is easy to determine if the 5 percent target was hit or not.

If a SMART goal was not reached, then these same twelve steps should be repeated. The causal factors for the shortcoming in results should be reexamined and the action plan scrutinized and modified as needed. The will to succeed is preceded by the will to prepare. Reexamining causal factors enables the crafting of different, more effective actions to implement to reach the desired results.

The stakes—enabling students' to achieve skills necessary to be successful in an ever-changing world—are too high to say "we tried but it didn't work." You aren't finished when you are defeated; you are finished when you quit. Great principals resolve to do whatever is necessary to make students successful. If the school improvement plan doesn't meet intended results, go back to the drawing board and make a new one.

12. *What is the best way to structure the school improvement plan?* Principals are advised to follow their district's template for a school improvement plan, if one exists. If one does not exist, then this one below, modified from the New York State Education Department, concisely captures all of the essential components to build a comprehensive school improvement plan.

The School Improvement Plan template below pulls all ten components of the plan together into one document:

1. Annual SMART goals are identified, for example:

   - Increase the percentage of students attaining mastery level on the end-of-course math exams as follows: grade 6—3 percent; grade 7—3 percent; grade 8—5 percent
   - Decrease the rate for chronic absenteeism from 11 to 8 percent or less for the 2020–2021 school year.

2. Summary of Causal Analysis Findings for the goals identified
3. Strategy or Strategies to achieve SMART goals
4. Objectives to be achieved in conjunction with the attainment of SMART goals
5. Activities/Strategies to achieve the SMART goals
6. Resources necessary to achieve the SMART goals
7. Timeline for achieving the goals. A clear target date focuses effort.
8. Responsibility/Involvement. Name a lead facilitator—this important decision specifies who is chiefly responsible for leading the work and other key people in achieving the SMART goals.
9. Monitoring Implementation. This entry states the plans for ongoing monitoring and adjustments to ensure that the SMART goals get met.
10. Specific Measures for achieving and documenting student academic improvement. This section describes additional actions the school improvement team will take to ensure that each SMART goal is achieved.

Table 5.3. School Improvement Plan Template (add rows as needed)

SMART Goal:	
Summary of Causal Analysis Findings: *(In the space to the right, summarize the major findings of your analysis of the reasons the problem exists and the effectiveness of current educational practices.)*	
Strategy or Strategies to achieve SMART goal:	
Objectives: *(Please write objectives as responses to the italicized questions.)*	*What school practices/programs will be improved through this strategy?*
	OBJECTIVE:
	How will student learning be improved/enhanced through this strategy?
	OBJECTIVE:

Table 5.3. (continued)

Activities/Strategies	Resources	Timeline	Responsibility/ Involvement	Monitoring Implementation	Specific Measures
What actions will occur? What steps will staff take? (Provide sufficient detail to ensure successful implementation of the activities).	What are existing resources that can be used? What new resources can be used?	When will this activity begin and end?	Who will take primary responsibility? Who else needs to be involved?	What evidence will be gathered on an ongoing basis to document successful implementation of this activity/plan?	How will student achievement and academic improvement be documented?

Principals are entrusted with much responsibility. Leading the creation and implementation of a school improvement plan is tremendously significant and satisfying work. It can raise the capacity of teachers to interpret data and craft solutions to problems. It can build confidence for the school within the internal and external school community. It can create respect for the principal. Most importantly, it can raise the skills of students. Press on.

References

Bernhardt, V. (n.d.). Five essential questions for starting school improvement right. Education for the Future, Chico, CA (http://eff.csuchico.edu).

Guido, M. (2018, October 19). 12 research-backed instructional leadership strategies. Prodigy (blog). Retrieved from https://www.prodigygame.com/blog/instructional-leadership-strategies/.

Mather, M. A. (2015, April 23). Causal analysis: Missing piece of the data puzzle? *Southeast Education Network*. Retrieved from https://www.seenmagazine.us/Articles/Article-Detail/ArticleId/4677/Causal-Analysis.

New York State Education Department. Comprehensive educational plan (CEP) for Upstate/Long Island schools and all charter schools 2011–2012. Retrieved from https://www.rooseveltufsd.org/cms/lib/NY01001495/Centricity/Domain/150/Centennial%20Ave_%202011-12%20CEP001.pdf.

Preuss, P. (2013). *School leader's guide to root cause analysis*. New York: Routledge.

University of Washington. Office of Educational Assessment. Understanding item analyses. Retrieved from https://www.washington.edu/assessment/scanning-scoring/scoring/reports/item-analysis/#:~:text=Item%20analysis%20is%20a%20process,the%20test%20as%20a%20whole.

Wagner, T. (2014, August 14). Leading for change: Five "habits of mind" that count. *Education Week*.

~

CHAPTER SIX

Leading Effective Teams

How to Hold Productive Meetings

Never doubt that a small group of thoughtful, committed people can change the world. Indeed, it is the only thing that ever has. (Margaret Mead, American cultural anthropologist)[1]

Principals sometimes try to accomplish all the work that needs to be done through their own efforts. However, it doesn't take long for them to realize that there is so much to do that they can't do it all themselves. The work of a principal is invariably accomplished by working with people. How can a principal effectively lead the work of teams? How can a principal ensure that participants believe that their time spent in meetings has been productive? This chapter describes a dozen ideas to answer those questions.

1. *Continually be resolute about improving the achievement of students.* If all of the principal's actions stem from a bedrock principle of improving the academic and social skills of students, then that principal will be respected and is likely to be followed. Such a philosophy should be continually evidenced by the principal's words and actions. If principals routinely and consistently take actions to improve the academic skills and the lives of students, they will be afforded respect. And such respect for the principal, who is obviously committed to improving the achievement of students, is fundamental to teachers being willing to devote time to meetings requested by the principal.

2. *Meet only if it is necessary to do so.* In contrast to Margaret Mead's inspiring quote to lead this chapter, American humorist Dave Barry wrote,

"If you had to identify, in one word, the reason why the human race has not achieved, and never will achieve, its full potential, that word would be 'meetings.'"[2] Undoubtedly, Dave Barry wrote that statement because he has squandered time at meetings.

Principals should always remember that everyone is busy and people don't like to waste their time. They should be respectful of people's valuable time and only convene meetings when necessary. If information can be gathered or disseminated via email, Google Docs, a survey, conversations, or any means other than a meeting, those methods should be used. Never hold a meeting simply because one has been scheduled. If there is no longer any need for a meeting to be held, cancel it. Much like not having to go to work on a snow day, people will be happy to have some time available to them that they did not expect to have.

Many principals find that an effective way of communicating ordinary but important information is through the use of a Monday memo or some similarly titled weekly communication. Such a weekly memo can list important announcements, upcoming events, deadlines, birthday greetings, congratulatory comments, and other ordinary occurrences.

Making such routine announcements via a Monday memo rather than taking up limited time at a faculty meeting or instructional-related meeting is a tangible way for principals to demonstrate that they are resolute about improving the achievement of students. Furthermore, eliminating routine announcements from faculty meetings enables principals to focus faculty meetings on instructional improvement activities.

3. *Meetings should have a clear purpose.* The purpose of meetings should be readily apparent to participants. Typically, the principal will set the agenda for the meeting, although participants could be asked to contribute agenda items to it. Creating a clear, meaningful agenda is fundamental to purposeful meetings, but it is just a start. Even if it is readily apparent by the agenda, a principal should stress the importance of the meeting and frame the important issues to be discussed during the introduction to the meeting.

Again, the meeting should attempt to address only those decisions that can be accomplished by holding the meeting. Having a clear, purposeful agenda whose importance is emphasized by the principal facilitates accomplishment of the agenda items and minimizes digression from the important tasks at hand.

4. *Be very purposeful about who should attend a meeting.* In general, four categories of people should be invited to meetings:

- Representative people who are well-respected by their colleagues
- People who have expertise or knowledge that will enable them to contribute to solutions
- People who are affected by the decision
- Informal groups (or power brokers) that may have an impact on change efforts

Using those criteria as filters will help principals to decide who should be asked to attend meetings. Most people don't want their time to be wasted and are okay with not being invited to a meeting if representative colleagues with expertise can act on their behalf. But, principals are wise to use these criteria in relation to their own school setting. For example, maybe only some teachers or parents can offer meaningful input on issues but, in order to build trust and/or increase transparency, it is best to invite all teachers or concerned parents affected by an issue.

Similarly, a principal may want to invite people to a meeting even though they don't have a role as a representative or have specific expertise to offer if those people are informal power brokers. Astute principals will seek to channel the energies of such de facto leaders into planning viable solutions to issues by involving them rather than leaving them on the periphery. Such local factors are examples of why decisions about who to invite to meetings must be made in the context of one's school environment.

5. *Be clear and up front about the team's authority.* Principals sometimes convene meetings and are perfectly fine with the meeting participants making final decisions on issues. At other times, principals want to hear the thoughts of meeting participants to gather an array of thoughts before making a final decision on an issue. Sometimes principals act as an ordinary team member with no greater authority than other team members and will accept a consensus decision.

Any of those options are fine. If the principal intends to allow the committee or team to make all the decisions on the issue, that should be stated. If the principal wants the team to be advisory and intends to make the final decision personally, that should be stated even before the team members meet. Tension and frustration comes when the authority of the team is unclear. Therefore, principals are advised to be straightforward with team members as to their decision-making authority *before* meetings begin.

6. *Start and end meetings on time.* As stated earlier, every productive meeting should have a clear agenda, including a starting and ending time. That means that the principal, as the facilitator of the meeting, should start it and

end it at the designated times. Some people arrive ten minutes before the meeting starts. There is no problem with that. Other people may trickle in 5–10 minutes after the stated start time of the meeting. Often, the person running the meeting says something like, "Well, it's seven o'clock. We'll just wait a few more minutes to see if anyone else is coming."

Two negative results occur if the meeting is not started on time. First, the people who were conscientious enough to arrive early or on time are penalized for their promptness by having to wait past the stated starting time. Secondly, the people who arrived late are rewarded for their tardiness because the meeting didn't start until they arrived.

Instead of delaying the start time of a meeting to wait on stragglers, principals should start the meeting on time by saying something like, "Thanks for arriving on time. It is now 3:15, so we will start." Those people who arrived on time will be appreciative that their time was valued and the meeting began on time. Those people who wander in late will miss something or perhaps feel akward for arriving after the meeting has begun. They will realize that you start meetings when you say you will start them and likely arrive on time thereafter.

Here is a "trick of the trade" that one veteran principal uses to get people to show up to meetings on time. She serves cookies or candy before the meeting starts, then puts them away at the scheduled start time of the meeting. People soon learn to show up before the meeting is scheduled to begin.

Similarly, many people have concerns that cause them to want to leave when the meeting is scheduled to end. They might need to pick up their children from day care, attend a graduate class, walk their dog, or any other variety of reasons. Therefore, they are appreciative that meetings end at the stated time rather than causing them to appear inconsiderate for leaving to attend to some other important activity while the extended meeting is ongoing. However, ending early is like a snow day—a welcome surprise.

7. *Structure meetings to enable productive participation.* The purpose of inviting people who have expertise, representative people, and people who are affected by decisions is to hear their thoughts on important issues. Oftentimes, though, meetings are monopolized by people who talk more than they should, who have a tendency to repeat their points, and/or who talk loudly. The result of such domineering actions is that more reticent people don't have an opportunity to participate in a meaningful way, if at all.

Principals should facilitate meetings by enabling all participants to offer their thoughts on the issues at hand. If such overbearing people are in a meeting, thereby preventing an open, flowing discussion, a principal may want to assume a more directive role by calling on people, in turn, until everyone who wants to speak has done so. That may necessitate, holding someone in abeyance while calling on others. A statement like this may be necessary, "Thanks for your thoughts, Chris, but we haven't heard from Dale yet. Dale, what are your thoughts on this issue?"

Power brokers tend to want to influence decisions. Principals must be keenly aware of that fact and conduct meetings where those people have a voice in decisions but do not wield undue influence. Principals are advised to communicate frequently with power brokers outside of actual meetings to understand their intentions and motivation to ensure that hidden agendas do not sabotage the official agenda of meetings or actions of the principal.

In addition to ensuring that everyone's thoughts are heard, it is also sometimes necessary to consider using formal roles such as a timekeeper or note taker. Doing so can ensure that sufficient time is spent on each meeting agenda item—but not too much time. Having a note taker can also ensure that all comments and actions have been accurately recorded.

8. *Frame issues as challenges instead of roadblocks.* Principals often hold meetings to decide upon important but somewhat ordinary decisions, such as making school safety plans, deciding upon curricular issues, scheduling personnel, creating the master schedule, or planning assemblies. All of the aforementioned points apply to such routine meetings.

Sometimes, though, principals have to hold meetings to address very difficult issues such as the impact of state aid being cut in the middle of the school year, an influx of English Language Learners, a significant loss of students due to businesses closing down, or a public health crisis like a coronavirus pandemic that requires schools to close. Even stronger leadership than normal is required for these very thorny issues.

Whether facing ordinary issues or extremely difficult ones, effective leaders must preach and model a CAN-DO ATTITUDE.

Sometimes the first few minutes of meetings devolve into a period of problem identification with statements similar to these. "How can we ever find a solution to this problem?" "We don't have enough funding to fix this." "We don't have enough time." "We never had any training for this" and similar statements which express people's genuine feelings.

Forward-thinking principals recognize that there is some value in letting people vent, allowing them to get their thoughts off their chest. Then, after a few minutes, they reframe the issue by saying something like this. "You are right. We certainly have plenty of obstacles facing us. But, let's look at them as challenges rather than roadblocks. Let's shift our thinking to finding ways to accomplish our goals rather than the difficulties facing us."

Such statements are not Pollyannaish. Time, money, and expertise are always limiting factors. But conscientious educators have historically found ways to improve schools despite insufficient funding, the limits of time, and the shortcomings of their current knowledge base. Indeed, people often embrace the challenge of solving difficult problems.

So, a principal must often be the chief cheerleader, the realistic but unwavering optimist who leads others in pressing on for the betterment of students and the school. Principals must try to create a sense of ownership in teams about solving problems and achieving goals. Doing so results in the team members having pride in their work and a sense of accomplishment for having worked diligently to achieve significant results—despite plenty of significant obstacles.

9. *Communicate well.* Communicating well is essential to leading effective teams and productive meetings. There are many components to communicating well. Here are some critical ones:

- Use data to identify opportunities for improvement. No one will support change for the sake of change. Cite and explain data so stakeholders will understand the compelling reasons for change and get behind finding viable solutions to issues. Use data to tell a story about why change is needed.
- Listen well. Be attuned to people's feelings as well as their statements. Don't respond right away when people say something. Simply be quiet for a few seconds. That pause will often result in people elaborating on their initial comments. Listening well and then restating someone's viewpoints demonstrates that you understand them. It also communicates respect for them. In turn, listening well to people and communicating respect for them results in respect for the principal.
- Principals should limit their own talking when leading meetings. There are four reasons for this. First, if principals want to know what others are thinking, they can't listen while talking. Secondly, if the principal expresses their own opinion on an issue rather than facilitating open discussion about it, some group members might withhold their opinions or thoughts out of deference to the principal by simply agreeing with the principal.

  Third, listening well communicates respect. No one respects a pompous principal who acts like he knows it all. Rather, a principal who genuinely seeks the thoughts of employees, students, and parents, regardless of their stature, is a person who earns respect. Fourth, hearing the opinions of team members may likely influence the thoughts and decisions of the principal. Soliciting the opinions of knowledgeable, respected stakeholders to help find solutions to issues is the point of holding meetings to discuss issues, after all.

Creating a culture where people without any authority are not only free but encouraged to share their thoughts on issues is a highly effective strategy for leaders who want a culture that informs their actions and enables them to be responsive to their constituents. For all of these reasons, to facilitate maximum discussion on issues, principals should hold off on expressing their thoughts until team members have shared theirs.

- Encourage *constructive* dissent. Leaders who truly want to know the thoughts of meeting participants will encourage people to speak their minds, even if the opinions proffered are contrary to what the principal might believe. Prudent decisions usually are not made by a principal listening to a bunch of "yes men." Principals, therefore, should overtly and regularly encourage people to truly state their thoughts in a constructive manner. Listening to such constructive dissent will communicate respect to meeting participants, convey an attitude of humility on the part of the principal, and, quite likely, result in better decisions being made.

- Let people know that their input was considered, even if it was not followed. If a principal follows the aforementioned actions, it is likely that many opinions will be given. It is also likely that not all of them will be the best course of action for the issues at hand. It is important, therefore, that the principal communicates understanding of people's opinions even if those recommendations did not translate into action.

To do so, a principal could say something like, "I've listened to all of the opinions and possible solutions to this issue. And I understand them (restate them to demonstrate an understanding of them). My decision on the issue is X for Y reasons. With a statement like that, the principal is, in essence, saying, "I understand you, but I don't agree with you." That is very important because people want to feel like their opinion was given full consideration even if it wasn't followed. And, they also can support decisions if a clear rationale for them has been articulated.

10. *Summarize and distribute the meeting minutes.* That is a pretty basic responsibility of leaders but it is worth noting because it is often overlooked. Even though teachers or support staff may entrust their representatives to represent them at a meeting with the principal, they still want to know about the actions taken at that meeting. An efficient way for leaders to distribute

minutes of meetings is to complete the minutes *at the meeting*. A principal could type notes on each agenda item or have a secretary or team member take the notes.

It is a wise practice to read the agreed-upon action before moving on to other agenda items to verify that all participants agreed upon the action as stated. Such a practice results in agreement on the minutes of the meeting before people walk out of the room, making it quite easy to send the minutes to everyone who may be interested in them.

11. *Be appreciative:* Everyone's time is limited. Principals must recognize that, by volunteering to attend a meeting or being a team member, people are not doing something else of professional or personal significance to them. Therefore, principals should state their appreciation to the team members for giving of their time. They should also publicly commend and thank them.

If it is appropriate during the meeting, do things to make the meeting enjoyable. Serve food. Use humor. Tape movie passes under some chairs and "award" them to the people who sat in those chairs. Give coupons for—a milkshake or certificates for a free lunch in the cafeteria, a desirable parking space for a week, etc. Meetings can't always be fun. More often than not, they are not. But, they should always be a worthwhile use of everyone's time. Showing appreciation is essential to recognize people who give of their time and talent. Having fun, if possible, is icing on the cake for being appreciated and doing significant work.

12. *Do a post-meeting analysis.* There are a lot of parallels between being a coach and a principal. After games, coaches do a post-game analysis. What went well? What didn't? "How could I have done a better job?" After meetings, principals might ask themselves, "Who fully participated? Who was reticent? Did someone monopolize the conversation? Did we digress from the issues? Did I do a good job of facilitating the meeting? Was I successful at leading people to reach consensus? What could I have done better?" In addition, principals could ask similar questions of team members either collectively or privately. Like a coach of a sport, self-scrutiny and seeking feedback from knowledgeable people improves results.

Leading teams and productive meetings are essential skills for principals. Principals would serve themselves and their school well by continually refining their skills necessary to do so. The aforementioned twelve points demonstrate the necessity of proper preparation for meetings, clearly communicating before, during, and after meetings, and showing respect and appreciation for participants.

Questions to Consider

1. Do the meetings I hold reflect my core value of improving the achievement of students?
2. Is a meeting the best way to get the information I need or can it be gathered without a meeting?
3. Are meetings well planned to achieve the desired results?
4. Are there sound reasons for the selection of meeting participants and do they know their authority?
5. Do I start and end meetings on time and have a clear agenda for them?
6. Do I facilitate well, enabling all people to have a voice while modeling a can-do attitude?
7. Have I done a thorough job of communicating about the meeting?
8. Have I shown appreciation for the time and effort people committed to serving as team members?
9. Have I done a post-meeting analysis to improve my skills?

Reference

Rogelberg, S. (2019, January–February). Why your meetings stink—and what to do about it. *Harvard Business Review.*

CHAPTER SEVEN

~

Creating Conditions for Success and Retention of Teachers

Strategies to Help Teachers Be Successful and Choose to Stay at Your School

> There are no good schools without good principals. It just doesn't exist. And where you have good principals, great teachers come, and they stay, they work hard, and they grow. (Arne Duncan, former U.S. Secretary of Education)[1]

Nearly every school administrator in the nation is well-aware of the shortage of appropriately certified and talented teachers. It is a problem that will exist for the foreseeable future. In fact, "The Economic Policy Institute, a nonpartisan think tank in Washington, DC, reports that the shortage of teachers nationwide from preschool through high school worsened from 64,000 in the 2015–2016 academic year to 110,000 just two years later (Garcia and Weiss 2019)." The agency projects the shortfall will reach at least 200,000 by 2025.

It behooves principals, therefore, to create conditions to retain the talented teachers that they already have. To do that, principals must be aware of the reasons teachers find the teaching profession dissatisfying enough to leave it entirely or at least disenchanting enough to leave one school for another. Stated more positively, they must be aware of what attracts teachers to remain in the occupation and also what influences them to choose to stay at their schools. The following table from the Learning Policy Institute (2018) identifies many of those factors.

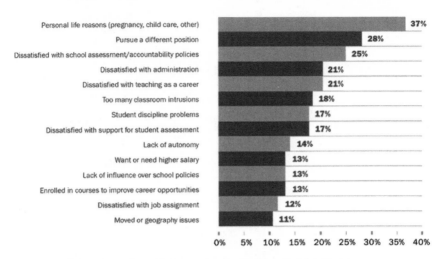

The percentage of voluntary leavers who rated the factor as extremely or very important in their decision to leave.
Percentages do not add to 100 because teachers can select multiple factors.

Figure 7.1.   Why Do Teachers Leave?
LPI analysis of the Teacher Follow-Up Survey (TFS), 2013 from the Schools and Staffing Surveys, National Center for Educational Statistics.

Really scrutinize that chart. Which of those factors does a principal have any influence over? What actions can principals take to encourage teachers' satisfaction and retention? How can principals help to create job satisfaction rather than job dissatisfaction? What conditions can principals control or influence that would cause teachers to flourish rather than become dissatisfied with their work? There are many tangible answers to those questions which we will explore below.

The following eighteen strategies to create conditions for the success and retention of teachers are divided into three broad categories: (1) Create positive working conditions that increase the skills of teachers, (2) Develop structures and practices to support instruction and learning, and (3) Treat teachers as professionals. Although each of the eighteen strategies falls into one of these three categories, the fact is that some of these strategies could go into more than one category. Categorizing them is not especially important. Following them toward the end goals of creating conditions that cause teachers to be successful and also choose to stay at your school is what really matters.

Create positive working conditions that increase the skills of teachers.
1. *Principals should hire for attitude as well as talent.* Obviously, teaching skills are critically important. Teaching skills can be assessed on the basis of past

performance such as student teaching or teaching at another school. A prudent and insightful practice to assess teaching skills is to have finalists for teaching positions teach actual lessons to students while being observed by the principal and interview committee.

But, a teacher with strong teaching skills who possesses a sour attitude or weak work ethic can turn kids off to learning and be cancerous to the morale of the school. When hiring teachers, therefore, look first for warmth, then competence. Many classroom management and instructional strategies can be taught to receptive teachers. However, it is very difficult to transform personalities.

Therefore, principals are wise to discern prospective teachers' affinity for students, passion for teaching, willingness to be team players, work ethic, attitude toward communicating with parents, and desire to continually improve their teaching competence to help ensure that they have hired teachers with the necessary personal attributes to be successful as teachers and as colleagues.

2. *Create a "family" atmosphere and welcome teachers into it.* After hiring teachers, principals should proactively welcome new teachers. Introduce them at faculty and department or grade-level meetings. Ask veteran, friendly teachers to watch over them and help them. Teachers new to the school or even veteran teachers in different departments or locations within the school may not know other teachers and might be reluctant to reach out to people they don't know.

Principals who continually build relationships with faculty and staff (a fundamentally important skill) likely know colleagues with similar interests and could introduce teachers with common interests to each other. If possible, create opportunities for teachers to interact with other teachers on a social basis such as by organizing breakfasts, luncheons, or staff volleyball games. Recognize accomplishments such as weddings, births, and attainment of graduate degrees.

Realize that teachers are parents and family members first, before they are teachers. To the extent possible, be flexible with issues such as them leaving early or arriving late to bring a child or elderly parent to doctors' visits. Even occasionally cover their class for them for a short period of time, if possible. Teachers will appreciate a principal's willingness to accommodate their needs and respect the fact that the principal is willing to take over teaching a class again. Such actions help to continually build a sense of a school-family for both new and veteran teachers.

3. *Create a collaborative environment focused on continual improvement.* A school led by a dictatorial, self-righteous, all-knowing principal will result

in an atmosphere of compliance rather than commitment, stagnation rather than improvement. On the contrary, a school in which the principal not only welcomes but encourages input from teachers about ways to do things better is a school that will continually improve because new ideas will be generated and supported.

Instructional and curricular practices, as well as the successful operation of schools, will be enhanced through open, respectful dialogue. In department and faculty meetings as well in ordinary conversations, principals should regularly seek the informed opinion of teachers about how to meet the needs of students and improve the school. New teachers with a fresh perspective may have some insightful ideas that could improve schools. More experienced teachers may have even more discerning ideas.

4. *Communicate clearly and respectfully*. A fundamental condition of a respectful, positive workplace is that teachers clearly know what is expected of them. Simply put, knowing expectations helps people to achieve them and minimizes the angst caused by confusion or uncertainty. Therefore, principals should be clear about expectations—for lesson plans, for pacing guides, the standards to be taught, for supervision of and interactions with students, who to go to with various concerns, when grades are due, safety drill procedures, ad infinitum.

If teachers need to be redirected then such redirection should be done in a respectful tone. Just like interactions with students, teachers should be treated with dignity and respect, even if their actions don't merit it. Principals should praise in public and redirect in private.

5. *Provide proactive support*. Teachers and other staff members appreciate being supported, even if they don't overtly seek support. They want to know that principals will help them with classroom management issues, teaching strategies, getting them needed resources, providing a buffer with difficult parents, resolving conflict with their colleagues, etc. To provide such support, principals need to develop relationships with teachers so that teachers feel comfortable asking for needed help.

Therefore, principals must be consistently proactive in developing relationships while simultaneously "checking the pulse" of the school. By making frequent classroom visits, principals can seek the concerns and opinions of teachers and also possibly observe any issues that may be troublesome to teachers or may be hindering the smooth operation of the school.

Another advantage of building relationships with teachers is that principals' relationships with veteran teachers sometimes allows those veteran teachers to feel comfortable communicating when they see that a new teacher needs support that a principal can provide. More eyes and ears are better for the school-community.

Visits by principals to classrooms of inexperienced as well as experienced teachers can occur during both instructional and noninstructional time. During those visits, let teachers know that you care about their success and that you are there to support them. Clearly tell them that you will help them with particularly troublesome issues. If teachers are having trouble with certain classes of students, principals should make occasional visits to those classrooms so that they will have a good grasp of the classroom dynamics. Moreover, their actions will demonstrate their desire for classroom success to both students and teachers.

Realize that teachers, especially new teachers, may be unsure of themselves and reluctant to share their concerns with principals. Be proactive about reaching out to them. Don't assume that no news is good news, especially with inexperienced teachers. Check in with new teachers every few weeks. Listen to their concerns and coach for success. Actions speak louder than words.

Develop Structures and Practices to Support Instruction and Learning
Principals should prioritize high-quality instruction and student achievement. There are a number of tangible actions that they can take to implement that philosophy rather than having it be a mere platitude.

1. *Assign new teachers to highly effective mentors.* Select mentors who will do everything possible to help new teachers be successful. Mentors can help teachers learn to manage student behavior, plan and deliver lessons, understand the operation of the school, make contacts, etc.

Being a good teacher is not enough of a criterion to be an effective mentor. Effective mentors must also possess a helping, caring attitude, a willingness to devote the necessary time to help an inexperienced teacher learn the craft of teaching, and a positive attitude toward the school. Pairing new teachers with a skillful mentor who also possesses a very friendly, helpful attitude is a tangible investment of time and resources toward helping teachers and students to be successful.

2. *Assign teachers a reasonable number of classes.* Teachers need to devote ample time to planning well and providing timely, meaningful feedback on students' work. Planning well, of course, helps students to master course content and minimizes disruptions. Feedback is so important to students that researcher John Hattie concluded that, "feedback was among the most powerful influences on achievement. Most programs and methods that worked best were based on heavy dollops of feedback" (Hattie 2009, 173).

Overloading teachers with too many class preparations may cause teachers to skimp on thoroughly planning instructional activities, teach fewer lessons that require higher-order thinking skills, require fewer assignments that require quality writing or analysis, and provide less quality feedback. Principals should regularly remind themselves that one of the main purposes of feedback is to help teachers assess the effectiveness of their instruction. Therefore, principals must create conditions that enable teachers to teach well and provide meaningful feedback by finding the right balance between the school's needs and teachers' interests and strengths before assigning classes.

3. *Avoid asking new teachers to take on additional assignments until they are highly effective teachers.* Principals often have a hard time finding extracurricular advisors or coaches and it is tempting to ask new, eager-to-please teachers to take on such a role. However, it is wiser to avoid asking new teachers to take on additional roles until they have proven that they can master their primary role of teaching.

4. *Provide instructional support and professional development.* Volumes of information have been written about professional development and principals are wise to seek current information about best practices from the numerous professional organizations cited in the chapter on "Leading instructional improvement." Three general principles about professional development are worthy of being considered as foundational principles for principals' to follow.

First, staff development is likely to be more effective if professional development needs are identified by the teachers themselves. Surely, there will be times when teachers need to learn information that is required by the school district. Beyond such instances, though, meeting the professional development needs of teachers by providing them with training they have identified and requested themselves is likely to be effective in meeting teachers' needs for skill development.

That premise leads to the second fundamental principle. Principals will experience greater success if they plan professional development in collaboration with teachers. That may be an obvious statement and a normal practice for many principals. But, it may also be a change in practice for some principals who think they know best, are reluctant to share decision making with teachers, or are accustomed to planning staff development activities without the input of teachers.

Teachers are smart people who want their students to succeed. When presented with test scores, disciplinary referrals, attendance data, or any other measure of school quality by principals, they can be productive partners in the process of planning staff development needs.

Such professional development should be closely related to the needs identified in the "School Improvement Plan." That is, once the school improvement plan has been identified, the next logical question is "What skills must teachers have to implement the School Improvement Plan?" Conscientious, forward-thinking principals and teachers can make productive professional development plans if they link teachers' PD needs with the school improvement plan.

Finally, principals should be aware that teachers are often more receptive to professional development provided by their teacher colleagues than someone from outside of the school. As stated above, many schools have many high-quality teachers who are respected by their colleagues. Having them teach skills to their colleagues is a low- or no-cost way to provide quality staff development. Principals are also wise to strategically assign instructional coaches, team leaders, or department heads to help teachers in need and standardize quality teaching practices and expectations.

5. *Create schedules that permit common planning time for teachers to collaborate.* There are basically two ways for teachers to collaborate to improve their skills. One is happenstance. By chance, teachers might have the same planning period. Maybe they bump into each other in the hall before or after school and share ideas. Or, perhaps they like each other and make time to share teaching strategies and concerns with each other. Of course, it is equally as likely that teachers who should collaborate to improve their skills don't have the same planning period, have schedules that cause them not to bump into each other, or don't like each other and so they avoid talking with each other.

The other way to cause teachers to collaborate to improve their skills is to actually create opportunities and schedules for such collaboration by creating the conditions that enable and require teachers to meet with each other. Principals at the elementary level can somewhat easily plan for teachers to meet by scheduling classes of the same grade to have specials such as art, music, physical education, and library classes during the same period. With careful planning, principals at the middle and high school levels can often create some common planning periods for subject-specific teachers.

The result of planning such common planning periods within the master schedule is that teachers can form professional learning communities or instructional leadership teams to share instructional strategies while simultaneously building camaraderie with their work mates. As mentioned in the chapter on instructional leadership, those meetings of conscientious, knowledgeable teachers to examine students' work and share effective teaching strategies hold the potential to increase the skills of all teachers.

That is especially so for new teachers who are still learning their craft. In almost any group of teachers, some will have skills that others do not. Some teachers may possess extraordinarily effective teaching or classroom management practices. Others may be very adept at using technology to enhance lessons. Others may know very useful techniques for causing student engagement. Some teachers may have successfully taught certain standards of learning or performance indicators better than their peers. By sharing their skills and strategies, the quality of a teaching staff can exceed the sum of its individual parts. Raising the skill level of teachers does not happen by accident. It must be planned.

A secondary benefit of those ongoing interactions during common planning periods is that an attitude is often developed that everyone in the school is responsible for the success of students—that grade-level or subject-specific teachers can and should help all teachers to be successful so that all students can be successful. Increasing teachers' skills and developing a "we're all in this together" philosophy are two compelling reasons to structure collaboration rather than leaving it to chance.

6. *Minimize noninstructional requirements for teachers.* Since teaching and learning should be the top priorities for principals, they should make schedules for teachers that minimize their administrative and supervisory duties to the extent possible. The work of the school must get done and some ancillary duties may need to be performed by teachers. Maybe condensing administrative and supervisory responsibilities and minimizing paperwork would significantly hinder the work of the school.

But, maybe there are more efficient ways of doing things that could enable teachers to devote more time to their essential work of lesson planning and providing feedback to students. A principal who desires to give teachers the maximum time to devote to instructional issues and respects the opinions of teachers will seek their thoughts about how noninstructional work could be streamlined or minimized.

7. *Conduct classroom observations to increase the teaching effectiveness of teachers.* All of the aforementioned practices can contribute to raising teachers' skills and students' outcomes, thereby causing teachers to want to stay in the teaching profession and at a school that provides such useful feedback. Another effective practice to raise the skills of teachers is conducting classroom observations of teachers.

The primary purpose of teacher observations is for principals to provide clear, tangible, constructive, helpful feedback and recommendations for improving teaching. Such observations should occur on a regular basis. By regularly observing teachers and providing useful feedback to improve teachers' performance, it will soon become apparent to teachers that increasing the skills of teachers is, in fact, the primary purpose of the observations.

Those observations could consist of walk-throughs that observe and comment on only a portion of the entire lesson. Or, they could consist of observing for an entire class period to gain a greater understanding of the context of the lesson and how the teacher teaches all components of it. Either way, frequent principal presence breeds more comfort with the principal being in the classroom and a feeling of that the principal is there to improve teachers' practice. Similar to a coach and player relationship, principals should be straightforward and diplomatic while giving direct, helpful feedback to help strengthen teachers' skills.

Evaluations differ from observations in that evaluations are less about improving teachers' performance and more about making a decision on renewal or nonrenewal. A principal who is only in the classroom once or twice a year is likely only there to evaluate rather than to provide ongoing coaching feedback to improve teachers' skills.

Time is always a limiting factor in principals getting into classrooms. In addition to the time-saving strategies cited in the chapter entitled, "Management precedes leadership," one very effective strategy to provide more meaningful feedback to teachers via classroom observations is to train other people in supervisory roles to conduct classroom observations. Doing so will both develop the capacity of other leaders within the school and offer more meaningful feedback to teachers than could be provided solely by the principal.

Assistant principals, department heads, and instructional coaches can become capable of observing teachers and providing constructive feedback to improve teachers' skills. Many teachers' contracts specify a minimum number of teacher evaluations and whether they should be announced or unannounced. However, if the purpose of an observation is to provide feedback to improve teachers' skills rather than to serve as an evaluation, there may be flexibility in who provides that feedback and how often it can be provided. Be sure to follow any applicable contract provisions regarding teacher observations and evaluations

8. *Require classroom visits to learn more successful teaching strategies.* Most schools are fortunate to have many successful teachers whose practices could be emulated by other teachers. In today's climate of shrinking state and federal financial support for education budgets, the money available for staff development may be decreased. More than likely, it will be insufficient.

Principals could raise the skill level of their teachers without spending any money to do so simply by requiring teachers to observe each other. Surely new teachers could fast-forward their success by observing the classes of successful teachers to learn classroom management, lesson-planning, and instructional strategies. In addition to providing mentors, principals could also structure schedules to enable veteran teachers to observe inexperienced teachers to provide them with constructive feedback.

Such observations of successful student management or teaching strategies may be particularly beneficial for new teachers, but they do not have to be limited to them. Again, most schools have many talented teachers whose practices could be beneficial even to veteran teachers. Remember that principals should endeavor to have high-quality practices become standard operating procedures rather than random acts of progress. Therefore, principals should collaborate with teachers to proactively structure classroom visitations so that the skills of all teachers can be enhanced and successful teaching practices become the norm.

Treat Teachers as Professionals

Teachers want to be respected and treated respectfully. If they are, then there is a much greater likelihood that they will stay in a school. If they are not, there is a strong chance they will leave one school for another or simply leave the profession for a more satisfying occupation. What, then, are actions principals should take to treat teachers professionally?

1. *Make shared decision making standard operational procedure.* Throughout this book, the advantages of involving teachers in issues that affect them have been advocated. That is because shared decision making results in better decisions being made in the first place, and those decisions enjoy much greater support than if they had been made solely by the principal since the people affected by them helped to develop them. In short, such involvement causes teachers to rightly believe that actions are being taken *for* them rather than *at* them.

Underlying the actions involved in participatory leadership is RESPECT. Tapping the expertise of teachers by giving them a voice in curriculum and instructional issues, forming the school improvement plan, planning professional development, and other school operational issues communicates respect for teachers. And, respect is one of the most important factors that cause teachers to stay in their positions.

2. *Involve teachers in crafting and implementing the school improvement plan.* Every school can improve and should establish a school improvement plan. The process of identifying student achievement goals and then accomplishing them would make sense even if development of such a plan were not required under the Every Student Succeeds Act.

Rather than being the primary architect of the school improvement plan, principals are wise to involve representative teachers in analyzing student achievement data and then setting lofty but attainable improvement goals. That process has always been vitally important. In light of the ongoing COVID-19 pandemic, it has become even more important as there are very likely gaps in students' learning caused by digital learning rather than face-to-face instruction.

After the school improvement plan is created, further respect can be shown to teachers by collaborating with them to develop strategies to achieve those goals. Next, it is also very important for the principal, in conjunction with representative teachers on the school improvement planning team, to decide upon strategies to communicate the school improvement plan and implementation strategies to the entire faculty.

3. *Allow teachers to express their interest in teaching assignments.* Teaching assignments are the responsibility of principals who must make such final decisions. But, if the needs of students are met (first) and the desires of teachers can also be accommodated (second), teachers will be pleased. They will believe they are treated fairly if their preferences are sought, even if they cannot be accommodated. Therefore, principals can meet the needs of the school and communicate respect to teachers as professionals if they create protocols for allowing teachers to identify their preferred teaching assignments.

4. *Provide teachers with autonomy and opportunities for growth.* Principals communicate respect for teachers when they provide autonomy for teachers in their classrooms. Teachers should be trusted to act professionally unless they do something to lose that trust.

Sometimes principals have a tendency to ask the most experienced, veteran teachers to serve on or chair a committee. Doing so is likely a pretty safe bet because veteran teachers hold the respect of their peers and will quite likely lead the achievement of the desired goal. However, always asking the most experienced teachers to take on leadership roles in the school also serves to limit the leadership potential of other teachers.

Principals can (and should) increase the capacity of their staff by asking people to serve in roles that will actually build their capability. Therefore, another way of communicating respect for teachers is to ask a variety of people to serve on committees or on task forces rather than just choosing the most experienced, veteran teachers every time.

Closely related to the notion of building capacity among all capable teachers is the practice of grooming highly competent teachers for leadership roles as appropriate. Many principals became principals because their principal saw leadership potential in them, put them in leadership roles, and encouraged them to pursue certification as a principal. Doing so is an important role of principals who are in the position to identify future leaders and involve them in leadership roles within the school that can strengthen their leadership skills.

5. *Involve teachers in the school budget.* Rarely will a school be allocated enough money to meet all of its needs. The budget development process is typically a process in which decision-makers decide the best way to allocate insufficient funds. Another way of treating teachers professionally, thereby causing them to feel respected and wanting to stay in a school, is to involve them in the school budget process.

Teachers selected for or asked to be involved in the budget development process should have the same mindset as the principal. That is, they must attempt to make budgetary decisions that have the greatest impact upon the most number of students while simultaneously meeting the needs of the school as a whole. Since resources are typically inadequate, it is a daunting and significant task.

Often, it is tempting to allocate an equal sum of money to all teachers. While that may be fair, it is often an entirely inadequate strategy to meet the needs of most students. Teachers' needs are not all equal. Generally speaking, new teachers, lab teachers, or teachers who use expensive technology or equipment may need more money than teachers who have been established in their classrooms for many years.

Principals and teachers who serve on the budget development committee must have the fortitude and wisdom to attempt to meet the needs of teachers by giving them the resources they need rather than giving all teachers an equal dollar amount. Allocating an equal amount of money for unequal needs simply doesn't make sense. It will surely result in some teachers receiving more than they need while others will receive an insufficient amount of money to meet their needs. Therefore, principals and representative teachers must distinguish between needs and wants to ensure that all teachers have the resources they need and the school prudently uses the limited resources available to it.

A way to do that which meets the needs of most teachers is the 1, 2, 3, budget request approach. Instead of allocating an equal dollar amount of the budget to teachers, principals could ask teachers to rank-order their budget requests, where "1" means it is essential; I cannot operate my class or program without this item. A rank of "2" means it is desirable; this item would substantially strengthen my class or my ability to fulfill my responsibilities. And a "3" means it would be an enhancement to my work; I could get by without it, but if there is extra money in the budget, I would like this item because it could augment my effectiveness.

Here are some final thoughts on creating conditions for success and retention of teachers and strategies to help teachers be successful and choose to stay at your school. Many students currently in high schools are experiencing much success and have great affinity for their schools. It is possible that principals could cultivate future teachers who will want to stay in their hometown school and community by encouraging such high school students to enter the teaching profession and return to teach at their alma mater.

At worst, such students may choose not to go into teaching and the principal's efforts will be for naught. But, at best, such encouragement might help develop a pipeline of talented, loyal teachers.

It is also possible that principals could work with universities which prepare teacher educators to enhance experiences in the areas of classroom management, instruction, and assessment, thereby making teachers more skilled as they enter the profession of teaching.

Those actions, while potentially beneficial, are not as significant in creating conditions that cause teachers to be successful and want to remain in a school as the eighteen important daily actions prescribed above. The impact of principals on teachers' job satisfaction can't be overstated. Principals are role models who establish the culture and practices of schools. If they establish practices that create positive working conditions which increase the skills of teachers, develop structures and practices to support instruction and learning, and treat teachers as professionals, then teachers will flourish. Teachers who flourish are likely to choose to stay at their school.

Principals who establish such conditions by going above and beyond what is required in their approach to daily tasks and relationships are likely to develop a school culture in which students are highly successful and teachers are happy. There is no traffic jam on the extra mile.

The following is a summary of strategies discussed in this chapter:

1. Principals should hire for attitude as well as talent.
2. Create a "family" atmosphere and welcome teachers into it.
3. Create a collaborative environment focused on continual improvement.
4. Communicate clearly and respectfully.
5. Provide proactive support.
6. Assign new teachers to highly effective mentors.
7. Assign teachers a reasonable number of classes.

8. Avoid asking new teachers to take on additional assignments until they are highly effective teachers.
9. Provide instructional support and professional development.
10. Create schedules that permit common planning time for teachers to collaborate.
11. Minimize noninstructional requirements for teachers.
12. Conduct classroom observations to increase the teaching effectiveness of teachers.
13. Require classroom visits to learn more successful teaching strategies.
14. Make shared decision making standard operational procedure.
15. Involve teachers in crafting and implementing the school improvement plan.
16. Allow teachers to express their interest in teaching assignments.
17. Provide teachers with autonomy and opportunities for growth.
18. Involve teachers in the school budget.

Questions to Consider

1. Do I know why teachers leave my school? Have I conducted exit interviews with them?
2. Have I created positive working conditions for teachers? What additional actions would be helpful?
3. Have I created conditions that increase the skills of teachers? What additional actions would be helpful?
4. Does my school have systems and processes in place to develop and support instruction and learning? What additional actions would be helpful?
5. Are teachers in my school treated as professionals? Would teachers feel they are being treated respectfully? How can I be sure? What additional actions would be helpful?

References

Carver-Thomas, D., and Darling-Hammond, L. (2017, August 16). Teacher turnover: Why it matters and what we can do about it. Learning Policy Institute.

Garcia, E., and Weiss, E. (2019, March 26). The teacher shortage is real, large and growing, and worse than we thought. Learning Policy Institute.

Gratto, J. (2015, April). Creating conditions for success for new teachers. New Superintendent E-Journal.

Hattie, J. (2009). Visible learning. New York: Routledge.

Lockett, P. (2019, November 11). To curb the teacher shortage, we need to think bigger about the problem. *Forbes*.

Podolsky, A., Kini, T., Bishop, J., and Darling-Hammond, L. (2016, September 15). Solving the teacher shortage: How to attract and retain excellent educators. Learning Policy Institute.

The role of principals in addressing teacher shortages. (2017, February 27). Learning Policy Institute.

Understanding teacher shortages: 2018 update: A state-by-state analysis of the factors influencing teacher supply, demand, and equity. (2018, August 24). Learning Policy Institute.

~

CHAPTER EIGHT

Motivating the Unmotivated

Getting Teachers and Staff Members To Do Their Best

True leadership lies in guiding others to success—in ensuring that everyone is performing at their best, doing the work they are pledged to do and doing it well. (Bill Owens)[1]

Unfortunately every school has them. Teachers and support staff who show up for work but seem to just go through the motions. Maybe, at some point in their career, they were eager and enthusiastic and did their best every day—but not now. Their heart doesn't appear to be in the job. Their attendance is in need of improvement and, often, so is their attitude. The result of their apathy is lackluster performance of their responsibilities and frustration for their colleagues. How can a principal motivate these unmotivated people? What would cause them to be motivated, to put their all into their position and carry it out with enthusiasm? This chapter will offer ten strategies to reinvigorate unmotivated teachers and staff members.

1. *Continually build relationships.* Like many other problems, the first step in finding a solution is to find the root cause of the problem. That can often be done by simply talking with (not at) unmotivated employees. People are likely to be straightforward with those with whom they have a relationship and reticent with those with whom they do not. The lesson for principals in this regard is to continually build relationships with employees so that they are willing to share their candid thoughts and feelings. Waiting until a problem has developed is not the best time to develop a relationship.

It can be done, though. Sometimes by listening to employees and finding solutions to their concerns, relationships are developed between principals and subordinates. But, a far better course of action for principals is to develop relationships on an ongoing basis. Continually talk with employees. Genuinely listen to their concerns. Listen some more. Get to know them as people, not just employees. Try to find mutual interests and common ground. If principals develop such healthy relationships, then addressing work performance issues can be approached more from the perspective of a caring colleague rather than an exasperated, heavy-handed boss.

In the chapter on "Preventing and addressing disciplinary issues," the premise is stated, regarding students, that "it is easier to prevent a disciplinary problem than to have to spend time dealing with it." In a similar fashion, it is better for principals (and the school) to motivate employees than to have to deal with the negative consequences resulting from their lack of motivation. A simple and effective strategy to do so is to sincerely pay attention to employees. The work of a principal is part art and part science. The "art" of the job is recognizing, encouraging, appreciating, and motivating employees, that is, building quality relationships.

There are other actions principals might take to prevent or minimize lack of motivation among staff. One of the easiest and most effective ways to build relationships can be accomplished through "management by walking around." In the classic management book, *In Search of Excellence*, authors Tom Peters and Robert Waterman Jr. coined the term "Management By Walking Around" (Peters and Waterman 1982, 289). That book was written in 1982 but the benefits of learning, listening, and building relationships by simply walking around and talking with employees are still valid today. Here's how it can work for school principals. In most schools a bell, a buzzer, or some other signal happens every 42 minutes or so, signaling the time to change classes. Whenever that signal occurs, principals should leave their desks and walk the halls. First and foremost, doing so prevents drowsiness. One can only sit for so long without getting logy. Most importantly, though, simply walking around the school is a very practical strategy to listen to and talk with teachers, staff, and students. Done consistently, a principal can develop many relationships.

2. *Express genuine appreciation for people's work.* No one wants to be treated like a replaceable widget or taken for granted. As noted in the chapter on "Leading effective teams," people want to be valued and appreciated, even for ordinary, daily work. A caring principal will thank people for their work, ask what help someone might need, and simply listen to employees' concerns. To quote Dale Carnegie from his classic book, *How to Win Friends and*

Influence People, "Be hearty in your approbation and be lavish in your praise" (Carnegie 1936, 54). Everyone needs to make money but money is not a motivator for someone to do their best. Rather, people respond to recognition, to heartfelt appreciation, and to thankfulness.

Principals are wise to minimize the likelihood of employees being unmotivated by following these preventative actions. Despite such actions, there always seem to be some employees on the bottom left side of the bell curve who still are unmotivated. What can be done to motivate them to do their best?

3. *Listen to determine the root cause*. As mentioned several times in this book, finding the root cause of a problem is an essential step in solving it. Sometimes teachers or staff members may have conflicts with their coworkers. They may be bored with their work. Maybe their ailing parents are consuming an inordinate amount of their time or their children are ill or have gotten into legal trouble. Sometimes teachers or staff members have drug, alcohol, or marital problems. Such issues are all too common. Many schools have Employee Assistance Programs (EAPs) that can help employees solve those problems. Principals can sometimes simultaneously build a relationship and help solve a problem if they know the source of the problem. Often empathetic principals who listen to their staff's concerns motivate employees to put forth much more effort in an attempt to please the principal who showed some concern for them. Once a principal knows the cause of an employee's lack of motivation, they can begin to find solutions to it. There are other ideas that might motivate the unmotivated.

4. *Address their needs or concerns*. If a teacher is bored and wants a different assignment or challenge, principals usually serve students and their school well to accommodate such requests, if possible. Likewise, mediating conflict between employees to make working conditions more pleasant and productive is well worth a principal's time. If teachers or support staff need supplies or resources, or more professional development to be successful, get them, if practical. Maybe the shifts of custodial staff need to be altered to enable employees to take care of elderly parents or young children. The point is that a principal who listens well and who probes to determine reasons for employees' dissatisfaction which results in decreased motivation, can often resolve underlying reasons that cause a lack of motivation.

5. *Appeal to their moral purpose*. Nearly every teacher became a teacher with the intent of helping students. Sometimes, reconnecting people to that sense of moral purpose rejuvenates them to serve students well, just like they originally intended when they went into teaching.

6. *Give people a new assignment to revitalize them*. Some teachers spend much of their career teaching at the same grade level or the same subject.

While tremendous expertise can be built by doing the same thing year after year, it is also a recipe for boredom. Such teachers may request a new assignment to alleviate their ennui. Principals who accommodate such requests often find teachers who become revitalized due to a new challenge, possibly working with more positive or forward-thinking colleagues, and a change of scenery.

If boredom or a been-there-done-that attitude is prevalent, then a principal has a solid reason to change the teacher's assignment, even if the teacher may be reluctant or unwilling to change. A principal should make decisions in the best interest of students as a bedrock principle. If it comes to a choice of doing what is best for students or making adults comfortable, then principals should clearly make decisions in the best interests of students. The same philosophy applies to support staff who might also get bored by doing the same job year after year. Any involuntary transfers should be made consistent with pertinent contract language.

7. *Be aware of the impact of group dynamics.* People of like minds often seem to find each other, whether positive or negative. Sometimes in schools, a group of negative people get together and oppress colleagues who have a positive attitude. Earlier in this chapter, the benefits of MBWA (management by walking around) were touted. Routinely being visible and sincerely being interested in employees results in principals continually developing relationships. MBWA, combined with relationships, enables perceptive principals to be aware of teachers who tend to be negative. Negativity can significantly damper enthusiasm and cause people to be unmotivated. It is very difficult to change personalities but it is certainly worth a try. More likely than personality transformation, though, is that principals can mitigate the impact of negative people and possibly reshape attitudes of negative employees by reassigning them to work with positive teachers.

If that doesn't work, then another option is to isolate teachers or support staff whose negative attitudes can decrease the motivation of other employees to do their best by placing them in assignments that afford minimal contact with the rest of the staff. That sounds pretty harsh and doing so should be a backup strategy if more positive efforts fail. Let's go back to the bedrock principle of making decisions in the best interests of students. If the pessimistic, whiny, griping, cynical, attitude of some employees is a causal factor in making other employees unmotivated, then their time available to associate with other employees should be restricted. Much like isolation and minimal contact between people is a strategy to prevent the spread of COVID-19, separating people whose destructive attitude might be caught by others is a tactic to help keep motivated, positive people from catching the virus of negativity and decreased motivation.

8. *Avoid the shotgun approach to confronting inappropriate behavior.* This point is not so much about how to motivate unmotivated staff as it is about how not to demotivate positive staff. Most teachers are nice people. When they move into the position of principal, they are still nice people—nice people who tend to want to avoid conflict. In almost every school there are staff members who don't take their responsibilities seriously and do unacceptable things such as arriving late to school or doing their jobs in a subpar fashion. Principals who want to address such inappropriate behavior but who want to avoid conflict sometimes will send an email to ALL staff reminding them to arrive on time, for example. The result of such a shotgun approach is that it does little to change the behavior of repeat offenders and it negatively impacts the morale of those people who do what they're supposed to do. Principals must have the fortitude and frankness to address offenders individually, eye-to-eye, in a professional manner rather than annoying people who are fulfilling their responsibilities.

9. *Make your expectations unequivocally clear.* If all of the efforts described above to turn an unmotivated employee into a motivated one fail, what is a principal to do? Unmotivated employees should be held to the same standards of quality work as motivated ones. They should not be worked around or held to lower standards because they are unpleasant to deal with. Principals should make their standards and expectations abundantly clear. It would be nicer for everyone if employees approached their work with a positive attitude. But, even if they don't, principals must still expect work to be done in a high-quality manner.

Make it clear that people will change or changes in people will be made. Doing substandard work is not an option. A principal cannot allow that to happen. Principals should continually monitor all aspects of the school's instructional and operational practices to ensure that high-quality work is being done on a routine basis. If people are unwilling to do high-quality work because they are unmotivated, then they must be replaced by someone who is enthused about doing the job well.

Perhaps principals could help such disgruntled teachers or support staff find other positions in the school or school system that would be a better fit for them and result in more satisfaction and success. Compassionate principals should try to do so. Maybe counseling-out employees is an appropriate course of action. Doing substandard work and fomenting negativity are not acceptable. Principals should make their expectations clear and hold all employees to them, even those who aren't motivated to achieve them.

10. *Document inappropriate behavior.* If teachers or support staff are unwilling or unable to do work in a satisfactory manner, then principals should follow the progressive discipline steps specified in their school district policies or contracts and "up the ante" by putting performance deficiencies in writing. Documenting substandard performance in an employee's performance evaluation or counseling memo makes it easier to deny tenure to an employee or perhaps even to remove the employee if there is documentation of enough infractions. Ideally, by clearly stating deficiencies and expected behavior in a counseling memo, that will cause substandard performers to see the light and meet performance expectations. If not, continue writing up specific shortcomings or infractions while clearly stating expectations to build the case for removal of the employee.

Unfortunately, some principals avoid conflict. Instead of addressing issues, they ignore inadequate performance or reassign poor performers to a different task to "hide" them. That lack of intestinal fortitude to confront a problem does a disservice to a school. It's also unfair and deflating to those who are doing their jobs properly. In the chapter on leading instructional improvement, it was noted that, "A school's results can never exceed the quality of its teachers" (Barber and Mourshed 2007, 16). A principal who knowingly reassigns an ineffective teacher to a different position to avoid conflict rather than pursuing removal of that teacher weakens their teaching staff. The same is true for a custodian or other support staff member who is not pulling their weight.

Furthermore, the long-term impact of keeping a weak teacher is that, over the course of years, many students are disadvantaged by having a weak teacher teach them. So, both the school and students suffer. The bottom line is that principals must use all tools available to get unmotivated staff members to either meet performance standards or remove them from their position.

Questions for Principals to Consider

1. Am I continually building relationships with all employees in the school?
2. Do I practice management by walking around? How could I improve my MBWA practices?
3. Do I build people's enthusiasm for their work by expressing genuine appreciation for them?
4. Do I listen intently to determine people's concerns about their working conditions?

5. Do I address those concerns effectively?
6. What are effective ways that I could create more positive working conditions for employees?
7. Am I astutely observing the impact of personal dynamics on employees' job satisfaction?
8. Am I making decisions in the best interests of students or adults?
9. Have I made my expectations about expected quality of work abundantly clear?
10. Are there ways I could help dissatisfied or unmotivated employees find more suitable work?
11. Do I consistently document substandard work?

References

Barber, M., and Mourshed, M. (2007). *How the world's best-performing school systems come out on top*. London: McKinsey.

Carnegie, D. (1936). *How to win friends and influence people*. New York: Simon & Schuster.

Heathfield, S. (2020, January 5). How to foster employee motivation. Retrieved from https://www.thebalancecareers.com/fostering-employee-motivation-1918745 .

Lipman, V. (2014, October 13). Four tips to motivate the unmotivated. *Forbes*.

Peters, T., and Waterman, R., Jr. (1982). *In search of excellence: Lessons from America's best-run companies*. New York: HarperCollins.

Powell, S. (2013, February 1). How to motivate the unmotivated. Retrieved from: https://leadershipfreak.blog/2013/02/01/how-to-motivate-the-unmotivated/.

CHAPTER NINE

~

You Can't Teach Kids Unless They Are in School

Ten High-Yield Strategies to Improve Student Attendance

So we all have a job to do. And we can do it together—black and white, urban and rural, Democrat and Republican. So often, the issues facing boys and young men of color get caught up in long-running ideological arguments about race and class, and crime and poverty, the role of government, partisan politics. We've all heard those arguments before. But the urgency of the situation requires us to move past some of those old arguments and focus on getting something done and focusing on what works. It doesn't mean the arguments are unimportant; it just means that they can't paralyze us. And there's enough goodwill and enough overlap and agreement that we should be able to go ahead and get some things done, without resolving everything about our history or our future. (President Obama)[1]

Principals today are under enormous pressure to improve test results. Those efforts are made much more difficult when students have poor attendance. It is hard to teach students who are not in school and those students, predictably, often produce weak results. Data from the U.S. Education Department, Office of Civil Rights, states that:

- Nationwide, more than 6.8 million students—or 14 percent of all students—are chronically absent (absent fifteen or more school days during the school year).
- More than 3 million high school students—or 19 percent of all high school students—are chronically absent.

- 23 percent of Black and 21 percent of Latino high school students are chronically absent.
- 21 percent of all English learner high school students are chronically absent.
- More than 3.8 million elementary school students—or 11 percent of all elementary school students—are chronically absent.
- Black elementary school students are 1.4 times as likely to be chronically absent as white elementary school students.

The Every Student Succeeds Act, signed into law in December of 2015, "Maintains an expectation that there will be accountability and action to effect positive change in our lowest-performing schools, where groups of students are not making progress, and where graduation rates are low over extended periods of time" (ESSA 2015, 1). That legislation has resulted in a renewed focus on improving attendance of students. As a result, many schools have made improving attendance part of their mandated school improvement plan under ESSA.

Aside from that push for accountability, there is a moral imperative to improving attendance of students. As illustrated in the chart below, the lower the education level, the lower the income earned over a lifetime and the greater the chance of being unemployed. Conversely, the greater one's

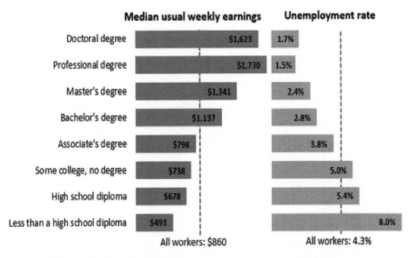

Note: Data are for persons age 25 and over. Earnings are for full-time wage and salary workers.
Source: U.S. Bureau of Labor Statistics, Current Population Survey

Figure 9.1. Earnings and Unemployment Rate by Educational Attainment, 2015
U.S. Bureau of Labor Statistics, Current Population Survey

education level is, the higher their salary expectations, and the likelihood that they will be unemployed is also reduced. High school dropouts will earn about $385,000 less than high school graduates and roughly $1,340,000 less than college graduates throughout their lives.

Conscientious principals must work to improve the attendance of students, particularly those students with chronic absenteeism. What are the root causes of poor attendance? Why do students drop out? Knowing the answers to those questions is fundamental to formulating plans to increase attendance. The organization, gradnation.org (Gould and Weller 2015, 1), has researched those questions and produced the following chart. The most common reasons students drop out of high school are heartbreaking.

Astute principals will ask, "Which of those factors can teachers at my school and I influence; what can my school do to mitigate those issues and cause kids to come to school regularly?" That is a worthy discussion for principals to have with teachers and other staff members. Greatly increasing attendance would also be an extremely worthwhile action for a school's improvement plan. See the chapter on "Crafting a school improvement plan."

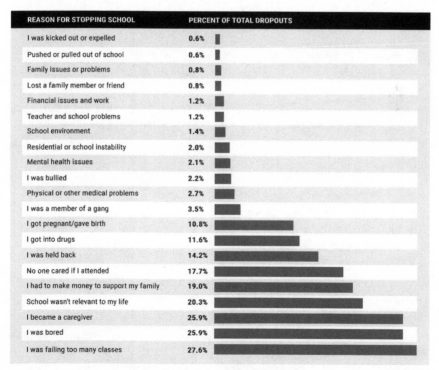

REASON FOR STOPPING SCHOOL	PERCENT OF TOTAL DROPOUTS
I was kicked out or expelled	0.6%
Pushed or pulled out of school	0.6%
Family issues or problems	0.8%
Lost a family member or friend	0.8%
Financial issues and work	1.2%
Teacher and school problems	1.2%
School environment	1.4%
Residential or school instability	2.0%
Mental health issues	2.1%
I was bullied	2.2%
Physical or other medical problems	2.7%
I was a member of a gang	3.5%
I got pregnant/gave birth	10.8%
I got into drugs	11.6%
I was held back	14.2%
No one cared if I attended	17.7%
I had to make money to support my family	19.0%
School wasn't relevant to my life	20.3%
I became a caregiver	25.9%
I was bored	25.9%
I was failing too many classes	27.6%

Figure 9.2.   The Top Reasons Students Drop Out of High School
GradNation.org

They will likely conclude that they have great impact over these factors:

1. Teacher and school problems 1.2%
2. School environment 1.4%
3. I was bullied 2.2%
4. I was held back 14.2%
5. No one cared if I attended school 17.7%
6. School wasn't relevant to my life 20.3%
7. I was bored 25.9%
8. I was failing too many classes 27.6%

The root causes of dropping out have been identified by gradnation.org. What strategies, then, could a principal take to change the culture and actions of a school to greatly increase attendance? Here are ten high-yield actions:

1. *Create a collaborative culture in which all teachers and staff purposefully develop relationships with students.* In the chart above, 17.7 percent of dropouts stated, "No one cared if I attended." That is an entirely preventable problem. As Dr. Seuss' Lorax puts it, "Unless someone like you cares a whole awful lot, nothing is going to get better. It's not" (Geisel 1971). Consider the illustrative story of the U.S. Education Secretary under President Obama, John B. King Jr. (Emma 2016, 1). When he was in the fourth grade, his mother passed away. Yet, he insisted on going to school *the next day* because he said his teacher, Mr. Osterweil, had a comforting classroom and conveyed caring about every student.

Education Secretary King said, "Lots of folks could've given up on me." "They could've said, 'Here's an African American, Latino male student. . . . at a New York City public school with a family in crisis. What chances does he have? But they didn't do that. They invested in me. They created this place that was compelling and interesting every day. Teachers gave me hope about my life and that's why I became a teacher." Stories similar to that could be told thousands of times because of the caring work of teachers, coaches, and principals.

Leadership matters when building relationships, particularly that of the building principal who sets and models expectations for students and staff. Principals should regularly inform their staffs of the critical link between relationships and attendance, set expectations for developing relationships with students, and model those expectations. For example, principals could set expectations that teachers greet students when they enter classrooms, call students by name, and proactively attempt to develop relationships with them. Teachers play a critical role in developing relationships. Coaches, advisors, bus drivers, cafeteria workers, secretaries, etc. should also be expected to take on the role of building relationships with students.

To further illustrate the importance of teachers developing relationships with students, consider the many school shootings that have been averted because students had enough of a relationship with teachers to alert them that another student was about to do something dangerous. The National Police Foundation (Langman and Straub 2019, 18) studied fifty-one school shootings that were averted and concluded that there is a:

> need to check in and maintain trusting relationships with students, even in the absence of direct warning signs of violence, multiple recommendations from the after-action reports . . . highlighted the importance of checking in with students and employees when it is clear they are in distress. Signs of distress include angry outbursts, verbal or physical aggression, inappropriate behavior, dropping out of a program, losing a job, or suing the institution. Recommendations addressing students' emotional needs appear in various forms among the after-action reports, including calling for a focus on improving school climate, engaging anti-bullying programs, strengthening relationships among students and staff, better integrating students into campus life, and increasing communication regarding students of concern.

All of those recommended actions are within the circle of influence of principals and further exemplify the significance of developing relationships with students. For most teachers and staff members, developing relationships with students is a natural, easy action. But some students are difficult to know or difficult to like. Therefore, it behooves a principal to continually remind teachers of the necessity of developing relationships with all students and to create conditions to do so. Like most other aspects of the school, the principal should lead by example and proactively develop relationships with students.

2. *Create a mentor program.* A mentor program can have ongoing positive effects because students will realize that at least one adult really cares about them. That could be enough to encourage kids to *want* to come to school. A mentor program is most effective when kids are matched with adults with compatible interests such as athletes with coaches, musicians with music teachers, video game enthusiasts with students who like video games, etc.

3. *Monitor attendance and follow up on students with weak attendance.* Monitoring attendance allows administrators to determine which students (and

parents) should be contacted. A good place to start would be to identify students who have the worst (25 percent) attendance record and meet with them and their parents to see how the school, the parents, and students can work together to improve attendance. Follow up on students who have weak attendance in face-to-face meetings and continue to hold conversations with their parents to try to improve students' attendance. Be diligent and persistent about getting kids to come to school.

Call every time a student is absent. Some schools have a policy of calling parents after a child has missed ten days or fourteen days. That is way too late. When students have missed that many days, they have developed bad habits that are difficult to overcome. They have become accustomed to easily missing school, making it even easier to continue missing school. There is also a good chance that they have fallen behind their classmates, thus providing a ready reason for missing even more school.

Unless there is a documented medical reason for the absence, calls should be made *every time* a student is absent. Does that take time? Yes. But, you can't teach kids unless they are in school. Being very persistent with phone calls to parents could be an effective strategy to get students in school. Automated calls to parents regarding their children's attendance can easily be ignored. Instead create a system to enable daily personal phone calls *from a caring school employee*. Callers should be "pleasant pests" who continually express concern for students and emphasize that good attendance is in students' best interest.

Principals can enhance attendance by talking with students, encouraging them to keep up good attendance patterns, and emphasizing how good attendance will help them. By greeting students who were absent the previous day with a simple statement like, "I noticed you were absent yesterday; I'm glad you're here today" students know that the principal cares about them and is monitoring their attendance. That personal expression of care by the principal is another tactic to increase attendance. It is even easier for teachers who have students in class to make such comments and they should be encouraged to do so.

4. *Minimize obstacles to attendance*. Again, it is necessary for a principal to know the root causes of a problem in order to solve it. So, delve into the reasons for absences. The better your relationship is with the student, the more likely they will tell you the reasons for their absences. Maybe kids are avoiding bullies, or they may be embarrassed about having shabby clothes or needing access to a shower. Perhaps they need childcare or are providing childcare. They may have an issue with alcohol or drugs. Perhaps they are struggling in some classes or experiencing conflict with a teacher.

The point is, principals must know the source of problems before they can be solved, so delve into the reasons for absences. The more a caring teacher or principal has developed a positive relationship with kids, the more students are likely to explain the reasons for their absences and welcome intervention to help them, thus resulting in better attendance.

Principals and the schools they lead must put a full-court press on improving attendance. Otherwise, these statistics from the U.S. Education Department, Office of Civil Rights, *and the real people behind them*, will continue:

- Number of high school dropouts annually: 3,030,000
- Number of high school students who drop out each day: 8,300
- Percentage of all dropouts that happen in the ninth grade: 36%
- Percentage of students from the largest fifty U.S. cities who graduate high school: 59%
- Percentage of U.S. crimes that are committed by a high school dropout: 75%
- Percentage of Black dropouts who have spent time in prison: 60%
- Percentage of Hispanic dropouts due to pregnancy: 41%
- Percentage of U.S. jobs a high school dropout is not eligible for: 90%

Source: http://www.statisticbrain.com/high-school-dropout-statistics/

5. *Create opportunities for meaningful involvement.* Take a look back at the definition of chronically absent students from the U.S. Department of Education stated above. To be classified as chronically absent, a student must be absent fifteen days or more during the school year. As stated previously, if someone misses that many days, it becomes easy to miss more. It becomes easy to slide down an unproductive slope of falling behind in classes, having weak relationships with teachers or classmates, and, in general, not having positive reasons to go to school.

In contrast to students who have no meaningful reason to attend school, "High school athletes earned higher grades, graduated at a higher rate, dropped out of school less frequently, and scored higher on state assessments than did non-athletes." That finding from a study comparing high school athletes to nonathletes in Kansas in 2008–2009 (Lumpkin and Favor 2012, 5) is likely true of athletes throughout the nation. Similarly, students who perform in band, chorus, theater, or who participate in virtually any other extracurricular activity have a positive, meaningful connection to school which will likely cause them to want to attend school. Therefore, school personnel would be wise to encourage, in fact—to push, involvement in extracurricular activities.

Look again at the chart above which showed these reasons for dropping out.

- No one cared if I attended school 17.7%
- School wasn't relevant to my life 20.3%

Principals should encourage coaches, drama directors, and music and cho-rus teachers to find a place in their sport or activity for students. Astute prin-cipals and teachers see themselves as missionaries to kids to save them from their circumstances or their own bad decisions. If they work with coaches and advisers to find ways to meaningfully involve students in extracurricular activities, even if it is being a manager for a sports team or being on a stage crew rather than being a star performer, then kids will be known and have a positive reason to go to school.

6. *Treat kids with dignity and respect—as if they were your own.* When stu-dents behave badly, punishment is typically warranted. It takes very little skill, though, for a principal to read the school discipline code and "process kids" by merely administering the specified consequences. Doing so handles the immediate issue but does not build relationships or cause students to be self-directed in a positive way. What would a principal do if the offending student were their own child? The principal would take time to listen to what's on kids' minds, including their frustration with classmates, teachers, or their families. Treating students like they are your own shifts a principal's thinking from administering consequences to helping students make produc-tive choices.

It takes more time to ask students what they would like to do with their lives—in school and beyond. Then, it takes even more time to discuss practical strategies to behave positively rather than do what they did to get themselves in trouble. There is an old adage, "Nobody cares how much you know until they know how much you care." When a principal demonstrates genuine, proactive concern for students, positive relationships are built which have the capacity to transform lives. Oftentimes, the result of such positive relationships is better decision making by students.

7. *Consider alternatives to suspension.* Sometimes the behavior of students is so egregious that it warrants in-school or out-of-school suspension. Such suspension may be appropriately consequential or may be necessary to make the school safer. But, what is the impact on the student who is suspended? That student is likely to learn less, fall behind academically, and be more likely to drop out. Wise principals consider the impact of suspension on the

student as well as on the operation of the school and sometimes consider these ideas instead.

- Whether students are suspended in-school or out-of-school, they are given the same schoolwork as their classmates and provided with tutoring consistent with state law.
- Other ideas to avoid or shorten suspensions include having students attend counseling sessions, for example, anger management; join a sports team; attend after-school extra-help sessions; voluntarily submit urine samples to verify that they are drug-free; perform community service; etc.

If warranted and practical, these ideas or others could be implemented to decrease the negative impact of suspension on students, build better relationships, and cause students to be more positive about attending school.

8. *Teachers should model excellent attendance.* The 2013–2014 Civil Rights Data Collection cited in this chapter also contained this finding under the heading: Chronic student absenteeism where the majority of teachers are also frequently absent. "Black students represent 15% of all students, but 21% of chronically absent students who attend schools where more than 50% of teachers were absent for more than 10 days." This data demonstrates that the attendance of teachers has a strong relationship to the attendance of students. Principals should encourage teachers to model the attendance they want from students. Of course, principals should also model excellent attendance.

9. *Tap community resources to help.* Oftentimes, the conscientious efforts of school personnel still don't result in a change in attendance for chronically absent students. Another tool to use to get kids to school is the resources within your community. Food banks, charitable organizations, local churches and shelters, or other community agencies can often provide help to people in need, thereby resulting in better attendance.

Maybe religious leaders could be enlisted to encourage people to have better attendance. A local appliance store may donate a washer and dryer to help kids have clean clothes. Enlist them as partners in your efforts. School nurses, counselors, or social workers often know sources of community help to meet the needs of students. Tapping such community resources is one more tool in the principal's tool belt to improve students' attendance.

10. *Use the juvenile justice system if necessary.* In most states, juveniles with chronic absenteeism can be referred to the state court system and have legal

pressure applied to them. For example, the process of putting a juvenile under the supervision of the court in Virginia is called the CHINS program or "Child in Need of Supervision" (Virginia Judicial System). This shortened definition describes many students throughout the nation. "A Child in Need of Supervision" means:

> A child who . . . is habitually and without justification absent from school despite the school system's reasonable efforts to effect the child's regular attendance without success . . . or
>
> A child who, without reasonable cause and without the consent of his parent, or guardian, remains away from . . . or abandons his family/custodian on more than one occasion.
>
> The "intervention of the court . . . to provide the treatment, rehabilitation or services needed" is sometimes a useful and necessary tool to change the behavior of students and/or their parents to improve attendance.

Using the criminal justice system should be a tool of last resort if the previous nine actions haven't resulted in excellent attendance for students. Nonetheless, principals should have the fortitude to use the juvenile justice system, if needed, if students or their parents fit the definition above.

Improving the attendance of students is critically necessary for their own good and for the good of the country. By developing positive, meaningful relationships with students and creating conditions for them to be successful, school principals and teachers are much more likely to help students improve their attendance and benefit from the many positive aspects of schools. Improving attendance is entirely doable with continual, persistent, focused efforts.

Questions to Consider

1. Have the students with chronic absenteeism been identified in your school?
2. What are the root causes of poor attendance?
3. Have the students whose attendance may become a problem been identified? Have mitigation efforts been implemented on their behalf? Are those efforts effective?
4. Does my school have an effective mentor program in place for students?
5. Have any obstacles for attendance of students been identified and removed?
6. Are students aware of opportunities to be meaningfully engaged in school? Do teachers and principals push students to join those activities?

7. Do teachers and administrators treat all students in your school with dignity and respect?
8. Are alternatives to suspending students routinely considered?
9. Are counselors, social workers, and administrators in your school fully aware of the community resources available to help students maximize their attendance?
10. Do you readily use the criminal justice system as a tool to help increase students' attendance?

References

Emma, C. (2016, January 8). King: Schooled by loss, 'saved' by teachers. *Politico*. Retrieved from www.politico.com/story/2016/01/king-schooled-by-loss-saved-by -teachers-217495.

Geisel, T., aka Dr. Seuss. (1971). *The lorax*. Retrieved from https://www.goodreads .com/quotes/4907-unless-someone-like-you-cares-a-whole-awful-lot-nothing.

Gould, S., and Weller, C. (2015, October 1). The most common reasons students drop out of high school are heartbreaking. *Business Insider*. http://www.business insider.com/most-common-reasons-students-drop-out-of-high-school-2015-10.

Langman, P., and Straub, F. (2019, February). A comparison of averted and completed school attacks from the police foundation averted school violence database. National Police Foundation. Retrieved from https://www.policefoundation .org/publication/a-comparison-of-averted-and-completed-school-attacks-from-the -police-foundation-averted-school-violence-database/.

Lumpkin, A., and Favor, J. (2012, March). Comparing the academic performance of high school athletes and non-athletes in Kansas in 2008–2009. *Journal of Sport Administration & Supervision, 4* (1). Retrieved from https://quod.lib.umich.edu/j/js as/6776111.0004.108?view=text;rgn=main.

Statistic Brain. (2017, July 17). High school dropout statistics. Retrieved from http:// www.statisticbrain.com/high-school-dropout-statistics/.

US Bureau of Labor Statistics. (2019). Retrieved from https://www.bls.gov/emp/ ep_chart_001.html.

US Department of Education. (2015, December 10). Every Student Succeeds Act (ESSA). Retrieved from https://www.ed.gov/essa?src=rn.

US Department of Education. (2016, June 7; revised October 28). 2013–2014 Civil rights data collection: Key data highlights on equity and opportunity gaps in our nation's public schools. Office for Civil Rights. Retrieved from https://www2 .ed.gov/about/offices/list/ocr/docs/2013-14-first-look.pdf.

Virginia's Judicial System. Retrieved from www.courts.state.va.us/courts/jdr/ Lynchburg/supervision.html.

CHAPTER TEN

~

Preventing and Addressing Disciplinary Issues

Free Up Time To Be an Instructional Leader

mishandling discipline can greatly affect a student's educational trajectory, or even more disheartening, the student's life. It is our duty as professional educators to realize that within every wrongdoing is a teachable moment. Further, we must take advantage of that moment rather than throwing it—and the student—out with the trash. Every behavior is a form of communication—even behaviors that require disciplinary action. Our responsibility as professional educators is to try to understand those behaviors and, simply put, begin to do better with our behavior management systems. (Weinstein and Maynard 2020, 9–10)

In the chapter on "Leading instructional improvement" it was emphasized that a school's results can never exceed the quality of its teachers. Therefore, it behooves principals to create conditions that cause teachers to continually improve their skills. One of the simple but overlooked ways of being an instructional leader is to help teachers minimize disruptive behavior and therefore spend more time on instruction. The more time teachers can spend teaching rather than redirecting inappropriate behavior by students, the more likely students are to learn. Equally significant, the less time the principal spends dealing with students who behave inappropriately, the more time the principal has for higher-order skills like observing teachers, conducting curriculum audits, monitoring professional learning communities, and other instructional leadership actions.

But, strategies to prevent and address disciplinary issues are usually not taught in administrator certification programs. The prevailing theory, presumably, is that handling disciplinary issues is common sense or that principals will learn effective strategies on the job. Both of those theories are logical. But every minute of the principal's day counts.

If one subscribes to the finding that "the quality of a school can never exceed the quality of its teachers," then it follows that the principal must devote the maximum amount of time to instructional leadership activities which help teachers enhance their skills. Therefore, the notion of spending minimal time on handling disciplinary issues so that maximum time can be spent as an instructional leader necessitates that principals actually know and implement effective strategies for preventing and handling disciplinary issues, and the sooner the better.

An ounce of prevention is worth a pound of cure is an age-old maxim. The corollary for principals is, "it is easier to prevent a disciplinary problem than to have to spend time dealing with it." With that precept as a philosophical basis, what actions can principals take to prevent disciplinary problems and the time spent dealing with them? This chapter presents ten strategies to answer that question.

1. *Look at the data to see if there are patterns.* Nearly every state requires that disciplinary data be maintained by schools. Such readily available data may inform inquisitive principals about where most inappropriate behavior occurs. Typical locations include school buses, in the lunch room, in locker rooms, in halls while students are passing from one class to another, in particular teachers' classrooms, etc.

Once patterns are discerned, then appropriate action plans to minimize those disruptions can be made. Maybe bus drivers need to be coached on how to develop better relationships with students. Maybe physical education teachers or coaches need to do a better job of supervising locker rooms. Maybe more or targeted hall supervision needs to be arranged. Maybe some teachers need help with classroom management. The point is that, once problem areas are identified and principals are armed with that knowledge, they can work with staff to craft viable solutions to minimize the reoccurrence of inappropriate behavior.

2. *Talk with the students who commit the most infractions.* Oftentimes, a small minority of students comprise the majority of disciplinary referrals. Sagacious principals who take the time to talk with those students may get to the root of the reasons why they act inappropriately so frequently. Several positive things can result from such conversations. First, caring principals can express a genuine desire to help those students be successful, thereby building positive relationships with them. Second, students may identify problem areas that the principals can help with. For example, sometimes the root of the

problem is conflict with students or teachers. Knowing that, the principal might help to resolve those problems. Sometimes students have been known to act out in class because it is "cooler" than admitting that they lack the skills necessary to be successful in the class. Equipped with that knowledge, a helpful principal can make plans to bolster such students' skills, etc.

Third, teachers will appreciate that the principal attempted to quell inappropriate behavior to enable them to have more productive teaching time. Fourth, if nothing else, those students may be aware that the principal is aware of their propensity for inappropriate behavior and may behave better as a result.

In addition to talking with students who commit infractions, it is also prudent to take notes about those conversations and the consequences administered for the inappropriate behavior. It is also helpful to take notes about conversations with parents about disciplinary issues. Those notes may be helpful to more effectively handle future interactions with students, or with parents who insist that it is the first time they've heard about their child's bad behavior (even though it may be your fifth conversation with them), or teachers who insist that you did not handle the issue appropriately. Also, many states require a comprehensive year-end report about the types of discipline issues that occurred at a school. Keeping accurate notes about disciplinary infractions and consequences enable that report to be completed as easily as possible.

3. *Implement "preventive discipline" strategies.* Principals are the chief drivers behind the culture of a school. Building a culture of continuous improvement and academic excellence should be at the forefront of every principal's agenda. Similarly, building a culture of "we are all in this together" and "it is every employee's responsibility to prevent disciplinary problems" will help to minimize such problems. Principals should lead by example in "preventive discipline" strategies such as walking the halls between classes. Despite leading by example, it is highly unlikely that the principal will be in the right spot at the right time to prevent every incidence of misbehavior. Therefore, creating a culture where all faculty and staff see themselves as responsible for preventing inappropriate behavior is a fundamentally important "preventive discipline" strategy. Doing so will multiply the principal's efforts many times over.

There are many more tangible actions that can be taken to implement a "preventive discipline" philosophy. Some of them are:

- *Ask teachers and staff to proactively develop relationships with students.* As mentioned earlier, "you can't teach kids unless they are in school" so developing relationships with students is a powerful factor in improving students' attendance. But, it is even more than that. Students are much less likely to behave badly with teachers whom they like and respect. Indeed, an observant principal will sometimes notice that students behave badly in some classes but not others. The reason for compliance in one class but not another can often be attributed to the teacher's relationship with students. So, building positive relationships with students is also key to effective classroom management.

- *Require comprehensive, engaging lesson plans for each class.* Engaged students typically do not misbehave. Principals who require comprehensive, engaging lesson plans for each class will have to handle fewer disciplinary referrals and see a greater percentage of class time spent on actual instruction rather than redirecting off-task behavior. Teachers can make their lessons more engaging by getting ideas from their principal, instructional coaches, team leaders, or department heads as well as by observing the lessons of successful teachers. In addition, best practices can be learned from the numerous professional organizations cited in the chapter on "Leading instructional improvement."

    If there is a pattern of referrals from particular teachers, it could be that the teacher has a class of immature hellions. Or, it could be that the teacher's lessons can be planned and delivered better. Both issues can be improved upon by discerning principals.

- *Assign supervision in common areas*—lunch rooms, bus areas, during the passing of classes, etc. Proximity to students decreases the chances of them behaving inappropriately. Much like assigning teachers to subjects or grades, it is essential to put the right people in the right positions for supervision. People who understand their role in building relationships, take their responsibilities seriously, and have enough fortitude to confront inappropriate behavior are the most effective in supervising common areas.

- *Have teachers or other staff sit next to students who are most likely to act inappropriately.* Chances are pretty good that teachers and principals know which students are most likely to act inappropriately in the lunch room, during an assembly, or in some other circumstance. It is a simple and obvious fact. Is it targeting students to have an adult sit next to them? Yes, and it helps activities run with fewer incidents, keeps kids out of trouble, and saves time for principals. Again, proximity to students decreases the chances of tomfoolery.

- *Teach appropriate behavior in situations that hold the potential for inappropriate behavior.* Appropriate behavior for the playground, lunch lines, emergency drills, assemblies, passing from class to class, etc. can be taught. Another old and accurate axiom is, "If you want it, teach it. If you get it, reward it."

These are just a few examples of "preventive discipline" strategies. By examining the locations and times of most disciplinary issues and collaborating with teachers in the trenches, principals are likely to develop many other "preventative discipline" strategies that can keep the school running smoothly, maximize instructional time, and keep students from making bad decisions.

4. *Require teachers to establish productive classroom rules.* Two basic, all-encompassing rules for students are recommended: (1) Don't do anything to impede the teacher from teaching and (2) don't do anything to hinder you or your classmates from learning. Many others could be added such as: Be seated and ready to learn before the bell rings, and treat everyone in this classroom respectfully. Teachers, could, of course, establish rules specific to their grade or subject. But if those first two are consistently emphasized as basic responsibilities of students, then many others are not needed.

Principals should regularly monitor teachers who are having difficulty with classroom management and provide them with tangible classroom management strategies. Have them observe teachers whose classroom management strategies are strong. Have such skilled teachers observe them and offer ideas. Two things will happen as a result. Those teachers will have a higher percentage of effective lessons—for the benefit of students. And your day will have less discipline issues to handle, enabling you to spend more time on instructional leadership issues.

5. *Have students "own" their behavior.* It is common for students to look outside of themselves for the reasons for *their* behavior. "He made me mad so I hit him." "Other kids cheat so I thought I could get away with it." "The teacher said something I didn't like so I swore at her," etc. Such statements indicate that students thought someone, other than themselves, was responsible for their actions. Wrong. Principals must continually emphasize that, no matter the circumstances or situation, students are responsible for their own choices, not someone else, and their decisions have consequences. While that is obvious to adults, it is not always so obvious to students. By teaching and continually reiterating that students make their own choices and they are responsible for them, students will come to accept responsibility for their own decisions.

6. *Go beyond the discipline code to help students be self-directed.* Some principals see their role regarding discipline rather narrowly. They think their

job is to simply maintain law and order by punishing students who behave inappropriately. Forward-thinking principals realize that handling disciplinary issues provides opportunities to help students become self-directed and self-regulated. They embrace the challenge of doing so because they realize that they are role models who have been entrusted with the tremendous responsibility of helping students learn how to successfully navigate school and life.

Virtually every school has a discipline code that specifies punishment for various offenses. If a student does X, then the consequence is Y. Following that code enables principals to "process" disciplinary referrals but it really doesn't take much skill to follow it. Anyone who can read moderately well can follow it.

Principals who see their role as mentors can help students to become self-directed by guiding them to examine how their actions affected them today and to consider alternative actions to help get them where they want to go in school and in life. Such discussions take much more time than merely processing students. After some time, those discussions result in changed values, attitudes, beliefs, and opinions on the part of students so that they become self-managed and forward-thinking rather than managed by a principal. Getting students to that point can help students tremendously. It can also be a source of great satisfaction for principals because they are doing work that will extend well beyond the walls of the school.

7. *Make consequences consequential.* The previous paragraph emphasized the importance of principals helping to shape new ways of thinking so that students can become self-directed. Principals should view disciplinary consequences as a tool to get the behavior they want—compliance with school rules and self-direction to help students achieve their best. Getting students to make decisions consistent with those objectives is the end goal; punishment is a means to getting there. But inappropriate behavior still merits consequences, not just talking about alternatives. Some disciplinary codes allow for no discretion by the principal. However, many give the principal some discretion. As a tool to help make responsible decisions more attractive to students, principals should use that discretion to try to find consequences for students that hold the potential to be sufficient enough to deter future inappropriate misconduct.

One such tool is the concept of progressive consequences. The first consequence for, say, being tardy to school is X. By explaining to students that the next consequence is X plus something more, some students will find the progressive consequence too unattractive and therefore behave in accordance with the school rules. Some students will not and principals should explain that they will get a progressively consequential punishment. Principals who explain progressive consequences to students can help those students think through the consequences of their actions and, hopefully, make better decisions rather than receive the increasingly severe consequence.

As an example, a simple but effective consequence could be time spent in a "thinking chair." Having a student sit at a desk placed facing a wall to the front and to one side, with a file cabinet on the other side makes for a rather unattractive setting for a student. If the student looks to one side, he sees a wall, straight ahead another wall, and on the other side, a file cabinet. Perhaps time spent in that "thinking chair," contemplating more appropriate courses of action, might prevent a repeat of the same behavior the next time the student is in the same situation.

If not, a principal could add additional time in the "thinking chair" the next time the student commits the same infraction. Putting the "thinking chair" in the principal's office or an adjacent room, where the principal can regularly engage the student in discussions about making choices that will help, not hurt, the student can be very productive. That is not always possible, of course, and principals surely want to avoid any situation where students get any bit of entertainment or satisfaction while being punished. If the principal's office is not an option, then having another responsible, forward-thinking adult monitor an unattractive setting could also work toward the end goal of getting students to think about more productive actions than the ones that resulted in them being in the "thinking chair."

A popular and effective consequence is restorative justice or restorative practices. "Restorative justice empowers students to resolve conflicts on their own and in small groups, and it's a growing practice at schools around the country. Essentially, the idea is to bring students together in peer-mediated small groups to talk, ask questions, and air their grievances" (Davis 2015, 1). Principals who use that philosophy and practice guide students to examine the consequences brought about by their inappropriate behavior and to repair relationships that were damaged because of that behavior. It goes beyond merely punishing students to cause them to "own" their behavior, examine the impact of their behavior upon relationships with fellow classmates or teachers, and to learn from the incident.

Another consequence that could deter inappropriate behavior is the concept of "adjournment in contemplation of dismissal (ACOD)." In legal parlance, here is how it works:

Adjournment in contemplation of dismissal (ACOD) allows a court to defer the disposition of a defendant's case, with the potential that the defendant's

charge will be dismissed if the defendant does not engage in additional criminal conduct or other acts prohibited by the court as a condition of the ACOD.
The defendant subject to the adjournment in contemplation of dismissal is
restored to the status he or she occupied prior to arrest, either during or after
the period of adjournment that accompanies the ACOD: that is, all records of
the arrest and after the period for which the ACOD applies . . .

The judge adjourning in contemplation of dismissal may impose specific conditions on the defendant subject to the ACOD, which may include community
service, drug rehabilitation, making restitution with a victim of the circumstances, avoiding contact with the victim, or completing some other diver-
sion program. It may also be accompanied by an admonition to abstain from
wanton, injurious, criminal, abusive or disruptive behavior. (Wikipedia.org)

If it is appropriate for the offense committed, the disciplinary history of
the student, and the policies of the school system, principals could use this
ACOD concept to structure a successful pathway for students. For example,
in lieu of a long suspension for students who got into a fight, principals might
shorten the suspension period if the combatants attend anger management
counseling (ideally run in-school by the school's guidance counselors or social workers). Similarly, drug-related offenses could be decreased if students
agree to attend drug counseling. Students who cheat on a test could receive
a lesser punishment if they agree to stay after school for extra help for some
period of time. What these ACOD ideas have in common is that they hold
the potential to make students more successful by keeping students in school
more often while requiring them to get the help they need.

Or, the write-up of an incident could be held in the principal's desk if
the student has no other disciplinary referrals within some specified period
of time. This ACOD strategy creates a condition that holds the potential to
keep students in school and prevent them from committing some other type
of infraction to avoid a more consequential disciplinary action.

8. *Swiftly and decisively take actions to keep everyone safe.* Keeping students
and staff safe is a fundamental responsibility of paramount importance for
every principal. Principals should take any necessary and appropriate preventative or reactive actions to keep everyone in the school safe and treated
respectfully. Being proactive by planning for safe conditions is preferable to
being reactive. Among other actions, principals should do whatever is necessary to prevent bullying and cyberbullying. For example, many people think
of Title IX as prohibiting discrimination on the basis of sex and requiring
schools to provide equal opportunities for students related to sports offerings.
That is correct. But Title IX also prohibits sexual harassment and sexual

violence; it also mandates that schools designate at least one employee to ensure compliance with Title IX—usually principals—who must promptly and thoroughly investigate any allegations of sexual discrimination, harassment, or abuse. Principals who follow these regulations keep students safe; those who do not jeopardize the safety of students.

From ensuring safe passage from class to class to investigating allegations of bullying and sexual abuse, principals must proactively and thoroughly analyze any situation where students' and staff's safety could be compromised. They must take proactive measures to prevent unsafe actions and aggressive action if unsafe behavior occurs.

9. *Allow students to save face.* Students who are sent to the principal's office for behaving badly often feel ashamed or angry. Most know that they have done something inappropriate and feel somewhat bad about it. They should be treated with dignity and respect—even if their actions were egregious. Keeping in mind that a fundamental purpose of discipline is to cause students to behave better, not just punish; principals can take several productive actions toward those ends when students are sent to their office.

- Give students time to cool down before addressing the issue. Tell them that you have to respond to a couple of emails before you can talk with them and wait a few minutes before talking with them.
- Play classical music on your computer loud enough for students to hear it and calm down.
- After a few minutes of the above actions, ask them what happened rather than accusing them of something.
- Listen intently for students' feelings as well as facts of the situation.
- Speak in a calm and monotone voice as much as possible. Doing so will keep the focus of discussion on what the student did. "A gentle answer turns away wrath but a harsh word stirs up anger" (Proverbs 15:1). Talk through possible options they could use if a similar situation reoccurs.
- At the conclusion of the discussion, build them up (if possible and appropriate) by telling them that you know they can make better decisions in the future and they can count on you to help them solve problems in the future.

10. *Involve parents—if they will be helpful.* Sometimes parents blame teachers or other students for their child's bad behavior. But in the majority of disciplinary cases encountered by principals, parents will complement and support the principals' efforts to redirect students' inappropriate behavior—if they are asked to do so. In most situations, parents like to be informed of

their child's misbehavior and the punishment meted out as a result. During those conversations, principals who are intent on improving behavior, rather than just punishing inappropriate behavior, will ask the parents to work with them in their efforts to help the student behave better. Phrases such as, "I am sure you would agree with me that you don't want Billy to . . ." or "Would you support my efforts at home to get Billy to . . ." are hard for parents to say "no" to. If parents are uncooperative, principals have a tougher job to teach students appropriate behavior. But if parents are willing partners, as most are, then a wise principal will enlist their help in teaching students to be self-managed learners.

One more strategy: Just as principals ask teachers to make positive calls home, principals can do the same. When students who frequently behave badly go for several days without doing so or make a good decision in a situation where they used to make a bad one, then principals could inform the parents of those good decisions. By doing so, a more positive relationship will be built with parents and they may reinforce those good choices with their child.

Collectively, these ten principles for preventing and handling disciplinary issues hold the potential to help principals to minimize time spent on handling disciplinary issues, thereby maximizing time spent on instructional issues, and helping students to become responsible students and future citizens.

Questions to Consider

1. Does handling disciplinary issues take up an inordinate amount of the principal's time at your school?
2. Does data regarding disciplinary issues reveal any patterns or trends? If so, what actions should be taken to address those issues?
3. What do the students with the most disciplinary issues have to say? Can their concerns be addressed to decrease their disciplinary referrals?
4. What "preventive disciplinary actions" are in place at your school? Would it be beneficial to implement any cited in this chapter? Would it be beneficial to implement additional measures?
5. Do all teachers practice productive classroom rules that result in minimal inappropriate behavior?
6. Do the people handling discipline issues at your school help students to realize that *they* are responsible for the choices they make?
7. Are consequences for inappropriate behavior significant enough to deter recurrence of such behavior?

8. Do the principals at your school act swiftly and decisively to keep students and staff at your school safe?
9. Do the principals' interactions with students who behave inappropriately allow them to save face and want to continue in school?
10. Does the principal partner with helpful parents to quell inappropriate behavior and teach self-regulation?

References

Adjournment in contemplation of dismissal. (n.d.). Retrieved from Wikipedia. https://en.wikipedia.org/wiki/Adjournment_in_contemplation_of_dismissal.

Davis, M. (2013, October 4). Restorative justice: Resources for schools. *Edutopia*. Retrieved from https://www.edutopia.org/blog/restorative-justice-resources-matt -davis .

Proverbs 15:1. A gentle answer turns away wrath, but a harsh word stirs up anger. Bible. New International Version. Retrieved at https://www.biblegateway.com/ passage/?search=Proverbs%2015%3A1&version=NIV.

Thorsborne, M., and Blood, P. (2013). *Implementing restorative practices in schools: A practical guide to restoring school communities*. London: Jessica Kingsley.

Weinstein, B., and Maynard, N. (2020). *Hacking school discipline: 9 Ways to create a culture of empathy and responsibility using restorative justice*. Highland Heights, OH: Times 10.

CHAPTER ELEVEN

Maximizing the Use of Your Time

Time Saving Principles and Strategies

> He who every morning plans the transaction of the day and follows out
> that plan, carries a thread that will guide him through the maze of the
> most busy life. But where no plan is laid, where the disposal of time is
> surrendered merely to the chance of incidence, chaos will soon reign.
> (Victor Hugo)[1]

Victor Hugo was a French poet and novelist, not a school principal. He
did not write about educational issues. His most famous works were *Les
Misérables* and *The Hunchback of Notre Dame*. But, perhaps he was thinking
about school principals when he wrote the words above, because they certainly apply to school principals. There is so much important work to do that
time cannot be squandered.

If principals are to carry out their many responsibilities in a highly effective manner, every minute of the day matters. Volumes have been written
about time management and readers can certainly find much more information about the topic from many books and articles. In the spirit of maximizing time, this short chapter will get right to the point by offering proven
principles and strategies to help principals achieve their priorities.

Principle # 1: Strengthening the Skills of Teachers Is a Top Priority for Principals' Time

Actions to Implement This Principle:

1. *Create conditions for teachers to collaborate.* Teachers possess a wealth of
knowledge about effective teaching strategies. Collaboration among them

holds the potential to increase the skills of other teachers as data is analyzed and successful strategies are discussed. But, such collaboration must not be left to occur by accident or happenstance. The key point is that principals must create structures for those productive discussions to occur by scheduling common meeting times, parameters for professional learning communities, and ensuring that those meetings are productive.

If they are productive, then teachers and students will be more successful, thereby enabling principals to spend more time continually leading actions to improve the school. Teachers could also plan some of the management or operational issues of the school. This topic is written about more extensively in the chapter entitled, "Creating conditions for success and retention of teachers."

2. *Schedule an abundance of time for teacher observations and feedback.* Principals should regularly schedule observations of teachers on their calendars, just like other meetings are scheduled: pre, actual, and post observations. Consider those observation times to be sacrosanct. It is rare that a principal will have to leave a classroom observation to handle some other issue. Most issues are not time-sensitive enough to cause a principal to leave during an observation. Make classroom observations a high priority and complete them unless there is a compelling reason not to do so.

When observing teachers, be sure to follow the teachers' contract and Board of Education policy regarding doing announced and unannounced observations. Generally speaking, announced observations enable teachers to thoroughly plan and prep students to behave appropriately for the observation. Such observations are generally not a true reflection of their teaching skills.

Unannounced observations are typically more representative of what happens in teachers' classes on a regular basis. In addition to doing as many unannounced observations as practical and warranted, principals should try to see each class or subject taught by teachers to form a clear, informed understanding of teachers' skills and provide constructive feedback to strengthen their skills.

3. *Help teachers with issues as needed.* If principals expect teachers to teach from bell-to-bell, then they must provide the help that teachers need, whether teachers ask for it or not. That might mean helping with classroom management concerns or providing help with planning engaging lessons. Principals should take away any reasons why teachers cannot be successful. In turn, teachers should work to remove any reasons why students cannot be successful.

Principle # 2: Set and Reinforce Expectations for Teachers

If the following high-quality expectations for teachers are clearly explained, communicated, and followed, then principals can save time by not having to deal with problems resulting from inadequate practices. Just as it is easier to prevent problems with students than to have to deal with them, the same concept is true with teachers and support staff.

Actions to Implement This Principle:

1. *Clearly communicate expectations of teachers for quality practices and standards of professionalism.* Such expectations could include modeling excellent attendance, arriving at school on time, dressing neatly and professionally, teaching from bell to bell, and preparing thorough lesson plans for substitute teachers. If expectations are clear, then minimal time has to be spent addressing issues caused by a lack of clarity.

2. *Establish expectations for quality lessons that include but are not limited to:*

- *Ensure that high-quality, standards-based lessons are taught* which include active student engagement, purposeful reading and writing, and generate enthusiasm for the subject matter. Following the many principles explained in this book about instructional leadership will help teachers to do so. Monitoring by principals is still advised.
- *Teachers should provide prudent assignments with timely, meaningful, constructive feedback* on them. Much like a coach or instrumental music teacher provide ongoing feedback, students' skills are strengthened when teachers provide plenty of cogent feedback to students on all aspects of their learning.
- *Objectives for each lesson should be posted and discussed prior to beginning instruction and students' understanding should be checked throughout the lesson.*
- *Make course expectations clear.* Teachers in middle school and high school should be required to post the syllabus for courses including methods of determining grades.
- *Treat students with dignity and respect.* If needed, teachers could be taught how to de-escalate kids rather than provoking inappropriate responses. (Confront in private, praise in public.)

3. *Decide who handles classroom management issues.* Time can also be saved by discussing with teachers, before students behave inappropriately, which student conduct issues merit the principal's attention or intervention and

which do not. Teachers should take the first shot at handling discipline issues and principals should get involved only if the teachers' efforts are not successful.

Principle # 3: Establish a Time-Efficient Working Relationship with Your Secretary

Highly competent secretaries can save a considerable amount of time for principals by solving many problems as well as by handling routine issues. Principals should collaborate with secretaries to forge a mutual understanding on common issues such as how to respond to people who may want to see you when you are out of the office, establishing a shared calendar so meetings can be scheduled for you, a protocol for knowing where you are and how to get in touch with you when you are out of the office, how to screen phone calls and visitors for you, etc. The following are typical actions principals could take to build strong, effective working relationships with their secretaries.

Actions to Establish a Time-Efficient Working Relationship with Your Secretary

- *Minimize phone calls.* Work with your secretary to decide which phone calls you should take and which should be routed elsewhere.
- *Minimize unplanned visits.* Do you have a minute? Work with your secretary to allow office visits only for an appropriate amount of time. Astute secretaries can tell people, before they enter the principal's office, that the principal is very busy and can only spend X amount of time with them before they have another obligation. If a person is long-winded, the secretary might interrupt a drop-in visitor by reminding the principal of a "meeting" she must go to or a phone call he must make in a couple of minutes to help moved the unplanned visitor along.
- *Make appropriate responses when the principal is out of the office.* Decide upon a thoughtful answer when people want to see you but you are not in the office, for example, "the principal is observing a class and should be back in about 15 minutes. I will leave a message for her to call you as soon as she is able." Or, "the principal is out of the office at a meeting until about 2:00 p.m. I will give her the message when she returns."
- *Prioritize mail.* Principals often have an abundant amount of mail to read. Secretaries can help them maximize their time by sorting mail into folders, for example, Red—essential, do now; Yellow—important; Green—get to when you can.

- *Communicate respectfully and continually.* Similar to a marriage relationship, the relationship between and principal and the principal's secretary must be continually worked on, with open communication, to make it highly effective.

Principle # 4: Create Routine Practices to Minimize Problems
Much is written about this topic in the chapters, "Management precedes leadership" and "Preventing and addressing disciplinary issues." Those chapters contain an abundance of information about how to minimize the time spent on routine issues and how to avoid time-wasting activities. It will be time well spent to read them again.

Actions to Implement This Principle:
1. *Resolve problems before they grow into larger issues.* Teachers and support staff members often have concerns about working conditions. Those concerns are often communicated through union officers or other representatives. Principals should regularly meet with leaders of teachers and support staff to listen to their concerns and problem solve with them rather than having unresolved problems fester. The axiom, "an ounce of prevention is worth a pound of cure," is quite accurate. The same precept is true with student issues at the middle and high school levels. Meeting regularly with students can enable principals to understand and be responsive to their concerns.

2. *Enlist parents in solving problems.* Meet with parents of students who consistently misbehave or have weak attendance to try to enlist their help. Discuss the root causes of ongoing bad behavior or poor attendance and address them, for example, conduct anger management counseling or social interactions counseling. Sometimes, parents can also work with their children to strengthen academic skills.

3. *Protect instructional time,* for example, by avoiding announcements during instructional time or bringing forgotten lunches, band equipment, or physical education gear to the office rather than to classrooms, etc.

4. *Be the backup for supervisory responsibilities.* Invariably, when you want to leave your office, that will be the time when someone pops in to see you or you get a phone call. Handling such issues often requires your immediate attention, thereby preventing you from fulfilling a supervisory responsibility. The people who have the primary responsibility for supervision usually appreciate it when the principal shows up and is supportive. But, more often than not, higher priorities occur and that is why principals should not schedule themselves as the primary person who does supervision duties.

Principle # 5: Solve Problems at the Lowest Level Possible

Actions to Implement This Principle:
1. *Ask parents to follow the chain of command.* Parents sometimes want to go right to the principal when they are upset about something with their children. But, more often than not, the teacher involved in the issue can resolve the problem. If parents call to tell you a problem with a teacher—ask the parents to try to first resolve it with the teacher. Tell them that, if they are not successful, you want them to call you back. Ask the teacher to call the parent. Set up the meeting if necessary. After a reasonable amount of time, follow up with the parent to see if parent-teacher concerns have been effectively resolved.

2. *Ask teachers and support staff to try to resolve problems at the lowest level possible.* Sometimes staff members have conflict with each other and they want the principal to resolve the issue. "Would you tell that teacher to pick up her students from art class on time?!" Principals should encourage teachers and support staff to resolve such issues by themselves and only get involved unless absolutely necessary.

Principle # 6: Delegate Effectively

Actions to Implement This Principle:
1. *Teach the skills necessary for someone to take on new responsibilities.* There are many potential leaders in schools. Principals can build capacity within them while simultaneously lessening their work load by following a few important steps.

2. *Delegate appropriately.* Make sure the person is willing AND knows the standard of quality you expect, such as date due, format, quality, etc. If appropriate, set benchmarks and timelines for completion of the project.

3. *Be a helpful resource.* Ask the person to whom you delegate what resources they need to be successful, for example, time, money, collaboration with colleagues, your help, etc.

4. *Monitor if necessary, but let it go.* By equipping, coaching, and enabling others to do quality work, their capacity for problem-solving and leadership increases. Having more such capable people in the school saves time for principals who must have confidence in the people they have designated to take on responsibilities.

Principle # 7: Maximize Your Time on Task and the Time You Spend on School Improvement Initiatives

Maximizing student achievement is a principal's highest priority. Therefore, principals should put first things first and intentionally align their actions with that core purpose while minimizing time-consuming issues that keep them from maximizing student achievement.

Actions to Implement This Principle:

1. *Set and achieve improvement goals.* Continually improve your school by setting and achieving clear goals for academic improvement. Focus your time on them. Do the top priorities well, rather than many things in a mediocre way.

2. *Continually increase your knowledge of instructional issues*—model being a life-long learner.

3. *Don't put off doing difficult or undesirable tasks.* Procrastination is the thief of time. Projects or paperwork will still be there even if you put them off. Resolve to get important work done in an efficient and high-quality way.

4. *Tackle difficult issues before easier, less-important issues.*

5. *Do one task through to completion before tackling another,* if possible.

6. *Avoid time wasters*—or at least minimize them. Minimize time spent on email and surfing the web, for example, limit pop-in visits to the office to a reasonable amount of time.

7. *Manage email effectively.* Responding to email can easily consume more of a principal's time than necessary. A few strategies can limit time spent on email. Look at the preview pane of the email to see if you even need to read it. If you do need to read the email, be deliberate about responding. Waiting a while to respond sometimes gives staff the opportunity to resolve issues without the principal's intervention. Waiting a while (a) may enable the principal to see a task to completion and (b) also reduces the expectation that the principal will immediately be responsive to concerns. Lastly, sort emails into folders so they can be easily found.

8. *Decide which issues you need to be involved in and when.* Not every problem or issue needs to involve the principal. Sometimes problems can be effectively resolved by asking the concerned parties to tackle the issue and bring their recommended solution(s) to the principal. Alternatively, other responsible leaders such as assistant principals, department heads, lead teachers, or instructional coaches can often handle issues in lieu of a principal, honing their own problem-solving skills in the process.

9. *Learn to say no.* There are so many meetings, conferences, and workshops to attend that a principal could be out of the office at them two to three days a week. Effective principals need to recognize what is essential versus what is desirable and focus on the task at hand by avoiding unnecessary meetings or conferences out of the office. Likewise, not every request to participate in a study or to take on a new project has to be honored. Sticking

to the business at hand of leading a school is plenty of work. Principals should be very judicious about any time commitments that impede them from successfully fulfilling their very significant role of continually improving their schools.

10. *Hold meetings only when they are needed.* Use a Monday memo or some other communication tool to communicate ordinary information. See additional information on this topic in the chapter on "Leading effective teams."

11. *Create a "Stop Doing List."* That term, coined by Jim Collins in his landmark book *Good to Great* (Collins 2001, 139), is sage advice. Analyze what things you do just because they have always been done. Are they in line with the goals of the school? Are they really important? What would happen if they weren't done? For example, is it necessary to attend *every* Child Study team meeting? Who could chair committee meetings effectively so that you don't have to?

Could your secretary compile the announcements and Monday memo or Friday letter rather than you? Could other members of the administrative team supervise some basketball games so that you don't have to attend all of them? Would it be effective to have your secretary write draft memos for you about routine issues that you proof and refine before sending them? Try to hone in on those things that require your time and attention and give up those things that others could competently handle.

Instead of just doing something because it has always been done ask yourself, "What one thing could I do to greatly improve X? Principals can also perhaps save time for teachers (and simultaneously gain their appreciation) by asking them what they could stop doing with minimal effect.

12. *Don't do something that somebody lower than you can do.* That sounds a bit arrogant but its basis is pragmatism, not egotism. Principals should not be arrogant. Instead, they should spend their time on fulfilling the responsibilities that *only* they can carry out. Lots of people can teach classes, set up computers, serve lunch in the cafeteria, do bus duty, etc. But, only the principal can carry out the duties of a principal and it is on those highly important issues that principals should spend their time. Therefore, principals should maximize their time by distinguishing those tasks that only they can do compared to tasks that other school personnel can effectively handle.

13. *Develop relationships with staff, students, and community members*—be visible, engage people in conversations. Attend as many events as practical. At first glance, developing relationships, being visible, and attending events actually sounds like it would take time, not save time. It does take time to do those things. But, the time spent building relationships at them by talking with people and showing a genuine interest in what is important to them

will pay dividends for principals. Having solid relationships with the school's constituents will make problem-solving, leading initiatives, and communication much easier, thereby saving principals a considerable amount of time.

14. *Analyze those things that consume your time and prevent you from working on your top priorities.* Is too much time spent on email or browsing internet sites? Do you put off difficult tasks? Do you have multiple projects underway at the same time rather than finishing one completely before moving on to the next? Find ways to minimize those issues that prevent you from using your time efficiently. Principals spend a lot of time solving problems they did not create. Such self-analysis helps principals to solve their own time-related issues as well as problems others cause, thus freeing up some time for themselves.

15. *Take time for yourself—take action to maintain your vitality.* Most people, especially leaders, need to permit themselves to enjoy time away from work. That time away allows them to be refreshed and rejuvenated. Principals consistently work hard but they don't need to be workaholics. Indeed, they are wise to spend an ample amount of time on other things that are important to them, such as their family, recreation, and spiritual life, so that they are well-balanced and model for their faculty and staff how to live a well-balanced life.

Rather than the people Victor Hugo was writing about, let it be said about you, "Every morning I plan the important transactions of the day and follow them through to completion. My plan keeps me focused on top priorities that guide my school to continually improve. Though busy, my actions and my focus lead me through the maze of a most busy life. I will not surrender my time merely to the chance of incidence. I will follow these principles and practices so that order and productivity, not chaos, will not reign."

Questions to Consider

1. Do I spend my time on actions that strengthen the skills of teachers?
2. Do I save time by setting and reinforcing expectations for teachers?
3. Have I established a time-efficient working relationship with my secretary?
4. Are routine practices in place in my school that minimize problems? Are there areas that could be improved upon?
5. Have I implemented practices and communicated expectations to solve problems at the lowest level possible?
6. Do I delegate effectively? How can I be sure? Am I building capacity in potential leaders?

7. Are there ways that I can maximize my time on task? What can I do to increase my productivity?
8. What can I stop doing to increase my effectiveness?
9. Are all the meetings I convene or attend necessary?
10. What are my biggest time wasters? Am I spending my time on what matters the most? How can I improve?

References

Collins, J. (2001). *Good to great: Why some companies make the leap . . . and others don't.* New York: HarperCollins.

Gratto, J. (2017, May). Out of the office and into the classroom. *Principal Leadership, 17,* 22–23. Retrieved from https://www.nassp.org/2017/08/07/may-2017-view point/.

Superville, D. (2018, October 16). "I want a job and a life": How principals find balance in all-consuming work. *Education Week.* Retrieved from https://www.edweek .org/ew/articles/2018/10/17/i-want-a-job-and-a-life.html.

~

CHAPTER TWELVE

Communicating to Build Confidence In You and Your School

Proactive Communication Strategies

The role of school public relations is to maintain mutually beneficial relationships between the school district and the many publics it serves. Each school district has its own unique way of carrying out this role, but there is one common element of all successful school PR programs: they are planned.

A well-thought-out, strategic communication plan will help ensure that a school district carries out its mission and meets its goals with the support of its staff and community. (NSPRA.org)[1]

Communicating well is just as essential and critical as building relationships in terms of importance for school principals. Communicating effectively can motivate the school-community to support continuous improvement efforts. Poor communication is likely to result in inconsistent messaging about what is important to the school, causing conflict and lack of support for school initiatives—both within the school and the community. Like building relationships, it can probably not be overdone. In fact, it is so important that the Professional Standards for Educational Leaders (PSEL) specifically states a standard related to communication:

Standard 8 of the Professional Standards for Educational Leaders is:

Meaningful Engagement of Families and Community: Effective educational leaders engage families and the community in meaningful, reciprocal, and mutually beneficial ways to promote each student's academic success and well-being. (NPBEA 2015, 16)

While that standard rightly addresses engaging families and the community, it is also highly important for principals to engage families and the community *within the school,* that is teachers and support staff.

Like many other school functions, effective communication does not happen by accident. It occurs as the result of thoughtful and consistent planning. This chapter will offer a dozen practical strategies for principals to successfully communicate with the families and the school-community as well as within the school.

1. *Communicate abundantly and redundantly through many sources.* Many issues that are the cause of conflict in schools or in the school-community typically have their origin in poor communication. Principals can and should deliver messages in multiple ways to meet the needs of people who seek information from different sources. For example the morning announcements (prepared by your secretary to save you time) can be emailed to teachers and parents, even students, so that everyone knows what is happening. A Facebook page, Twitter account, and newsletters should all be standard means of communication.

Ordinary information can be posted on the school's web page to avoid answering routine questions such as about upcoming events, news items, student and staff accomplishments, directions to other schools for sporting events, etc. Doing so will minimize the time you and your secretary spend answering predictable questions.

It is also essential to communicate with community members who do not have children in the school. That population is often a majority in many communities and they tend to vote more than younger people. In states that require voter approval to pass school budgets, bonds, and referendums, their support is crucial. Therefore, schools must continually give them reasons to vote "yes" by communicating school improvement plans, awards, events, and the many other good things that are happening within the schools.

If the principal does not create and shape communication about the school, who will? The disgruntled person who did not get hired for a position at the school? The local gossip on a Facebook page? The person who runs the barber shop or beauty salon? Communicating abundantly and frequently enables the principal of the school to distribute accurate information about the school rather than someone who may have an axe to grind or be ill-informed.

2. *Be the school's chief promoter.* Continually highlight students' successes in routine communications. Talk about accomplishments and works-in-progress. Post your goals widely throughout the school and on the web page—let everyone know the school's priorities and that yours is a school that is continually improving.

In addition, actively seek opportunities to promote the school. Invite yourself to speak at civic organizations, the PTA or PTO groups, etc., to share the school's story. In essence, shape the narrative about the good things happening at the school.

3. *Communicate professionally.* Administrators are held to a high standard. When speaking with students and staff, words and body language matter. Even though they may think or feel otherwise, principals should always act professionally with students, teachers, staff members, and parents.

Teachers and parents also expect principals to produce professional, error-free communications. The quality of their communications establishes expectations for teachers and staff. Therefore, principals should strive to consistently produce clear, cogent, error-free written communications.

Here are a few ideas to help principals do so. Before sending an email or a letter, take the time to proofread it several times to ensure that it is error-free. Spellcheck does not catch words that are spelled correctly but are the wrong word. Reading a letter or email aloud to yourself is an effective way to make sure that is written exactly as you want it.

Another simple tactic to help principals consistently produce error-free work is to hold off on putting a name(s) into the address line until you have fully proofread the email. That prevents an email from being inadvertently sent before it has been thoroughly proofread.

When speaking with internal or external groups, write an outline of the key points you want to make. If you are still gaining expertise and comfort as a public speaker, practice as much as necessary beforehand. Never read your PowerPoint slides. Most audiences read well and can read the slides themselves. Reading slides does not add to one's presentation. Rather, it bores the audience. Instead, use points on the slides as key informational points or cues and elaborate upon them from your depth of knowledge on the topics.

4. *Communicate efficiently.* Succinct messages that are direct and to the point are most helpful to busy teachers and parents. If you are sending out a daily email, be sure to include things that are of the utmost importance— schedule changes, room changes, upcoming events, etc.

Using Monday memos or a similar weekly tool to communicate routine information enables principals to (a) communicate important information and thereby (b) reserve faculty meetings for higher priorities such as staff development. Communicating efficiently also helps to ensure that your messages actually get read by busy parents and teachers.

If it is possible and practical, allow parents to opt into the type of news they wish to receive from the school, such as individual classroom updates, athletic updates, theatre or music news, school system news, news about extracurricular activities, etc. When teachers or staff members other than the principal are controlling such news, be sure to stress to them that they are representing the school and must communicate with utmost professionalism.

Principals gain support by connecting with their audiences, not by trying to impress them with their knowledge. Communicating professionally and efficiently requires speaking and writing in ordinary, understandable language to the target audience. Avoid acronyms and jargon that may be common to educators but are lost on laymen.

5. *Be responsive to concerns.* As principals practice "management by walking around" (MBWA) and building relationships, they are likely to learn issues that are of concern to teachers, students, and parents. As a result, they can proactively communicate to address those issues. For example, newsletter, web page, and Facebook articles could include columns entitled "Did you know?" or "Your questions answered." Perception is reality. Through proactive, rather than reactive, communications, principals can help shape the perspectives of internal and external stakeholders.

Similarly, principals can and should anticipate questions that will be asked about programs or procedures and proactively answer those questions. A question-and-answer format is effective for doing so. Another simple and effective way to be responsive to parents is to return phone calls, within the same day if possible but no later than 24 hours. If parents are concerned about something enough to call the principal, then the principal needs to alleviate that concern as soon as possible. The same advice goes for teachers who should also be required to return phone calls to parents within 24 hours.

More often than not, when parents call the principal about a classroom concern, the teacher can resolve the issue with the parent. As a routine practice, principals should inform the parent that they will have the teacher call the parent to address the issue. Most teachers will do so satisfactorily. But, a minority of teachers will neglect to call the parent or will deal with the parent in a brusque, dismissive way. After delegating parental concerns to teachers, principals should be sure to place a follow-up call to parents a day or two after the issue has been raised to ensure that it has been satisfactorily resolved by the teacher.

One additional way to be responsive to parents and the community is to have a real person answer the phone instead of an impersonal voice directing callers through a series of options. Being responsive is always important. An area where schools often fall short in being responsive is during the summer months when many schools operate with shortened "summer hours." Community members are often resentful of school employees who work ten months and then possibly become even move resentful when employees work less than a full day in the summer and a call to the school is not answered in the afternoon.

If "summer hours" are a tradition in your school, then a way to still be responsive to community members is to stagger the shifts of people so that there is always a person answering calls during all normal business hours. These collective actions comprise responsive, customer service.

6. *Create opportunities for two-way, face-to-face communication.* Giving parents opportunities for two-way, face-to-face communication is an excellent practice for school principals. Enabling parents or community members to express their concerns directly to school leaders demonstrates respect for them. Simultaneously, it enables principals and their key staff to understand problems or concerns—which is the first step in rectifying them. Parents and community members often have useful ideas that can strengthen the smooth operation of the school or can help students achieve more.

There are many ways principals could implement two-way communication activities. Some of them are as routine and easy as attending PTA or PTO meetings on a regular basis. Other routine activities could be advisory meetings. Depending upon the size and needs of your school, those advisory meetings could range from a general advisory committee about all school issues to parent advisory committees for English for speakers of other languages (ESOL), before- or after-school childcare, special education, gifted and talented students, etc.

Some principals hold a "Conversation with the Principal" on a monthly basis. Those meetings have no agenda other than for the principals to listen to concerns of parents and respond to them. Principals could bring assistant principals or other key personnel with them, such as the athletic director or department heads, to respond to questions. The time of meetings could be rotated every month to accommodate the different schedules of parents. For example, one month the "Conversation with the Administrators" could be held in the morning and the next month it could be held in the afternoon or early evenings.

Some principals hold a Saturday morning, "Coffee with the Principal" every month or every other month. That is a big time commitment for principals but one which puts huge deposits into the emotional bank accounts of parents who respect the fact that principals have taken time away from their personal lives to listen to their concerns.

An excellent vehicle for two-way communication is a "Key Communicators Organization." To form one, principals could invite the president (or their representative) of key organizations to meet with them on a regular basis. Monthly meetings work well.

Those key communicators could be drawn from whatever organizations are affected by the school—the chamber of commerce, business owners, clergy members, the presidents of sports leagues, the library director, the mayor or town supervisor, the president of the local taxpayers group, the teachers' union, etc. The principal could bring any other key administrators to the meeting who might be beneficial. The monthly meeting should be convened in the school with light snacks and beverages.

Following this three-item agenda can generate much confidence in the school:

1. Any questions about the school can be asked; *any questions are fair game*. Such willingness to tackle even very difficult questions demonstrates the principal's honesty and openness.
2. The principal can *inform the key communicators of any issues the school is currently facing*. If desired, the principal could seek thoughts about them from the key communicators. Informing the key communicators of current and upcoming issues keeps them in the know about such issues and demonstrates that the principal is forward thinking. The key communicators may also feel a bit special because they have been asked to contribute ideas to strengthen the school. Most importantly, the key communicators can spread accurate information about the school to the many people with whom they interact, thus building confidence in the school.
3. The principal could *ask the key communicators if they have information they would like to share with other key communicators*. Oftentimes, community organizations may have complementary goals but may be unaware of what other organizations are doing or how they might be helpful to each other. Sharing information about upcoming projects or concerns may cause beneficial collaboration.

Within a couple of days following each meeting, the principal could send minutes, summarizing concerns expressed and the actions taken, to all key communicators. For example, key communicators might ask questions like, "What percentage of students who graduate from this high school attend two- or four-year colleges? What is the dropout rate? What percentage of minority students take Advanced Placement classes compared to white or Asian students? How many middle school students take Accelerated courses?"

A principal may not know such specific information at the meeting. But, by getting back to key communicators with accurate answers to those questions, the principal communicates respect for the questioner and transparency about the school.

Well-informed teachers and staff members can be tremendously effective ambassadors for schools. Therefore, internal communications with teachers and staff, such as by using some type of weekly internal newsletter, is a fundamentally important practice. In addition to regular communication coming from the principal, principals are well-advised to also make the time for two-way communication with teachers and support staff members on a routine basis.

In addition to MBWA, principals could take the same concept explained in the "Conversation with the Administrators" above and hold routine meetings with teachers and staff members to understand what is on their minds and keep them informed about important information.

7. *Involve people in issues that affect them*. Much has been written about this principle in the chapter on "Creating conditions for success and retention of teachers" as well as the chapter on "Crafting a school improvement plan." Involving parents and community members in issues that affect them is just as important for them as it is for teachers. It is a simple premise. People are not likely to support something that they do not understand.

Conversely, people are more likely to support something that they do understand. They are even more likely to support something that they had a part in creating. Principals who sincerely involve parents and community members help to create a mindset that the school is "our" school by meaningfully involving parents and community members in issues that affect them. In the process, they will likely make better decisions which will enjoy greater support.

Standing advisory committees may be sufficient for most issues involving general input. Depending on the issue, involvement could be expanded to a committee or task force with a specific charge, such as planning pick-up and drop-off areas for students, developing a new report card, or establishing a sports hall-of-fame. More complicated issues such as revising school attendance zones might involve many community forums initiated by the central office.

Again, as educated, wise, and conscientious as principals may be, their ideas still need to be supported. Support is created by genuine involvement. A decision-making process that involves people in issues that affect them is likely to generate more effective solutions to concerns that will be better-supported because of that involvement.

8. *Be a source of helpful information for parents*. Schools are filled with wonderfully knowledgeable, conscientious teachers, administrators, and

counselors who hold a wealth of information that can help parents. By anticipating parents' concerns and needs, schools can help parents successfully help their children.

The possibilities for school staff to help parents is almost endless. Teachers could send home information about how to help their children become more proficient in reading, writing, and math. Information could be provided about how to help children complete homework, become enthusiastic readers, and prepare emotionally for state tests; additionally, information could be offered regarding kindergarten registration, extracurricular opportunities, graduation requirements, how to prevent bullying and cyberbully, dealing with stress, how to select a college and complete the college application process, programs for dealing with drug or alcohol issues, preventing date-rape, and on and on.

By having a mindset that schools educate the whole child and that the school and parents are partners in the process, schools will continually find ways to collaborate with parents in that process of helping children become successful in school and beyond. The following poem illustrates this point well.

Unity

I dreamed I stood in a studio and watched two sculptors there. The clay they
   used was a young child's mind, and they fashioned it with care.
One was a teacher; the tools she used were books and music and art. One was
   a parent, with a guiding hand, and a gentle, loving heart.
Day after day the teacher toiled, with a touch that was deft and sure; while
   the parent labored by her side and polished and smoothed it over.
And when at last their task was done, they were proud of what they had
   wrought. For the things that they had molded into the child could neither
   be sold nor bought.
And each agreed she would have failed if she had worked alone; for behind
   the parent stood the school, and behind the teacher, the home.

—Cleo V. Swarat

9. *Record and post videos of significant information.* Principals and their staffs continually try to share information such as routine matters, updates on curriculum and instructional issues, and safety procedures. Despite their importance, busy parents often have childcare or work issues that prevent them from attending open houses or other school functions and will miss that information if it is communicated only at school events. That can cause

parents to miss valuable information and/or principals and their staffs having to repeat it.

A tool to help communicate important information accurately and minimize time spent repeating it is to simply to record videos of important information and post them on the school's website. Likewise, videos could be recorded by other key staff members who communicate important information. For example, the director of special education could record information about the special education eligibility process and the parents' role in forming individualized education plans.

Athletic directors and coaches could record videos about expectations for athletes, etc. Such proactive communication would enable parents to access information on their time schedule and likely save time for the principal and other key administrators by preventing them from having to repeatedly communicate the same information.

10. *Survey stakeholders.* Surveys can be tremendously beneficial for principals as a means of being responsive to school stakeholders. Students, teachers, support staff, parents, and community members all have opinions about the school. First and foremost, surveys to determine their satisfaction with the schools demonstrates respect for the people who take them. Astute principals can then take information gleaned from such surveys to implement improvement efforts.

When surveys are regularly administered *and* followed by resultant school improvement initiatives, schools continually improve and respect for them and their leadership grows. Like all of the other communication initiatives mentioned in this chapter, administering surveys can also be done for no cost by cash-strapped schools by using free survey sites such as Survey Monkey.

11. *Communicate clearly and abundantly in crisis situations.* Ensuring that students and staff are safe is a fundamental responsibility of paramount importance. Principals should, of course, take every measure they can to ensure everyone's safety. Despite the best efforts of schools, unsafe conditions sometimes occur in schools, such as COVID-19, the MRSA virus, swine flu, dangerous weather conditions, students with guns, etc. In such crisis situations, principals must be pillars of strength and provide clear, factual information.

Principals should anticipate the need for clear communication in a crisis and build the necessary infrastructure and databases to communicate before a crisis occurs. When a crisis does occur, principals may want to prepare press releases, write fact-sheets, communicate information via Twitter or Facebook, and update web pages. The more that principals can do to clearly state the facts of situations and the prudent steps they are taking to ensure everyone's safety, the more confidence people will have in the school.

The same points apply to any school issue that is likely to be controversial or that requires widespread, speedy communication. Another common maxim is, "Proper planning and preparation prevents poor performance." That axiom can be applied to many aspects of school leadership. But it is particularly apropos when applied to the need to accurately and broadly disseminate information when communicating rapidly is essential.

12. *Bad news doesn't get better with time. Be forthright about it.* There is no perfect school. Tests scores may be subpar. Students may behave badly or do something dangerous. Attendance may be too low and the dropout rate too high. Teachers sometimes behave inappropriately. Budget shortfalls are all too common, etc. It may be tempting for principals to sugarcoat such issues or not report them at all.

But, bad news doesn't get better with time. And a principal's credibility is essential to their success. So, rather than ignoring negative news or trying to put a positive spin on it, principals will gain respect by simply stating the facts of the situation. People appreciate and respect honesty as opposed to deceptiveness. In conjunction with reporting the facts of a situation, principals should also report their plans to address the issue. Doing so can cause them and their school to be viewed as proactive problem solvers rather than deceitful laissez-faire administrators.

This list of a dozen communication strategies provides some practical ideas to implement a "customer service" mindset. Principals who follow these steps and who are genuine and transparent in their communication actions will help to create much public confidence in their schools.

Questions to Consider

1. Does my school have effective methods to communicate to internal and external stakeholders?
2. How are my own communication skills? How can I improve upon them?
3. Are my written communications clear, succinct, and error-free?
4. Am I responsive to the concerns of students, staff, and parents? Are teachers?
5. Are there opportunities for staff and community members to engage in two-way communication with the principal? Should more opportunities be created?
6. Do I routinely involve people in issues that affect them?

7. Do I use surveys to gauge the perceptions of students, staff, and parents as a school improvement tool?
8. Are procedures, such as videos posted on the school's website, in place to communicate routine information?
9. Are plans in place to communicate in a crisis situation?
10. Am I forthright in my communications?

References

Gratto, J. (2015, March 10). Schools and parents are essential partners in the education process. MultiBriefs: Exclusive. American Association of School Administrators Executive Briefing. Retrieved from: http://exclusive.multibriefs.com/content/schools-and-parents-are-essential-partners-in-the-education-of-students/education.

———. (2018, March). 10 Take-charge actions for effective proactive communication. *Principal Leadership*, *18*, 20–21. Retrieved from https://www.nassp.org/2018/03/01/march-2018-viewpoint/.

National Policy Board for Educational Administration (NPBEA). (2015). Professional standards for educational leaders. Reston, VA: Author.

Swarat, C. V. (n.d.) Unity. Public domain.

CHAPTER THIRTEEN

~

Master Communication and You Manage Conflict

Tips for Preventing and Dealing with Conflict

[C]onflict resolution skills are crucial to your success and personal growth. Everybody experiences conflict throughout their life. Conflict happens because everyone is unique. We all interpret and communicate ideas differently, and we don't always have the same priority or point of view. Conflict can be looked at as unhealthy and harmful, and it can often stress us out and lower our productivity. However, when we use conflict to develop better understandings with those around us, it can be a positive experience. That is because conflict can teach you a lot about yourself and give you tools to use in your daily life (Shaw 2019, 1).

Despite one's effort to avoid it, conflict comes with the territory of being a principal. Students behave badly, and worse yet, their parents sometimes blame teachers for their children's poor or inappropriate behavior. Too often, teachers behave inappropriately and their behavior must be confronted. Colleagues might be cantankerous. Supervisors might be unreasonable. The sources of conflict are many and ongoing. What is a principal to do to minimize conflict and deal with it when it occurs? Let's start by examining actions principals can take to avoid conflict in the first place.

Actions Principals Can Take to Avoid Conflict in the First Place
1. *Communicate abundantly and redundantly.* As stated in the previous chapter, "Communicating to build confidence in you and your school," frequent communication is a great way to build confidence in and respect for the school. Such ongoing, repetitive communication is also a terrific way to

avoid conflict with the school's stakeholders. When people feel ill-informed or when they expect something and another thing happens, they get frustrated with the person they think was responsible for communicating accurately in the first place.

Principals can avoid, or at least minimize, the angst caused by inadequate communication by communicating and then communicating some more. People go to different sources to gather information. Therefore, a principal is wise to communicate in as many venues as practical—the school's web page, Facebook, Twitter, parent portal, newsletters, the school calendar, etc. In addition, principals could send the daily announcements to parents via email.

The superintendent and other superiors don't need to know about everything that occurs in schools but they should surely be apprised of issues that are controversial and will possibly end up on their desk. Oftentimes, disgruntled staff members or parents will think that they can get what they want by bypassing the principal and going right to the top of the organization. They don't hesitate to call or email the superintendent.

Superintendents want principals to be successful and can typically help them resolve issues and defend them if their actions are reasonable. But, they must be fully apprised of the issues to do so. Therefore, it is incumbent upon principals to keep their superiors fully informed about any issues that someone who is dissatisfied with the principal might bring to them.

2. *Be consistently fair and student-centered in your actions.* People get justifiably upset if they feel someone is given preferential treatment. Principals must consistently treat all employees, students, and parents fairly and impartially. The strategies cited in the chapter entitled, "Creating conditions for success and retention of teachers" are excellent reminders of actions that engender respect for principals rather than conflict.

Fundamentally, if actions of principals are in the best interests of students, it will be difficult for people to take issue with them.

3. *Address resistance head on.* Principals often know who is opposing them, talking about them, or likely to be resistant to their initiatives. Rather than letting discontent foment, principals could allay their concerns by talking directly with such people. Finding the sources of their frustration and addressing them is a very effective way of mitigating conflict. Don't take it personally when people disagree with you, which they will do often. They may be looking at issues from a more narrow perspective than you. If you are making decisions in the best interests of students, you will likely have peace of mind, even if others disagree with you.

Many administrators are not so good at not taking things personally. Their feelings are hurt or they become angry and defensive when maligned. While that may be natural, it is not helpful in resolving conflict. As difficult as it may be when attacked, principals can "keep their cool" by following these strategies:

- Examine your own motives. If you have been fair, truthful, forthright, and made decisions in the best interests of students, then you can have peace about the decision that caused conflict. Again, realize that critics may be looking at the issue from a narrower perspective based upon self-interest whereas your lens for making decisions is all students and the best interests of the school.
- Sometimes people are just plain mean and/or want to impugn people, like a principal, who are successful. Even though you may be boiling inside, it will be gratifying not to let them get any satisfaction from seeing you get angry or upset by keeping a steady, impassionate demeanor.
- Remember that it is likely very important to maintain a positive relationship with the offender. Responding with corresponding vitriol will probably harden someone in their position and make a working relationship quite difficult in the future. More about this topic is stated below in the sections entitled, "Disagree without being disagreeable," "Keep the focus on the issue rather than the other person's inappropriate behavior," and "Be a role model at all times."
- Taking a few seconds to gather your thoughts before responding is an effective strategy to avoid saying something you might regret later. Remember, the only person whose behavior you actually control is your own, not anyone else's. So, be sure to act with dignity and respect even though you may feel disrespected and it may be difficult.

4. *Be media friendly.* Principals can cultivate positive relationships with members of the media by continually giving them positive news stories about the school. Even if bad news occurs, be straight with the media rather than trying to evade questions. It is easy and respectful to give reporters copies of presentations and complete details about issues. Such demonstrable respect for reporters is likely to be reciprocated by reporters who, in turn, will treat principals fairly and respectfully.

Conversely, if such respect and cooperation with the media is withheld, then principals can expect disrespectful treatment in turn. See more about communicating effectively in the chapter entitled, "Communicating to build confidence in you and your school" and be sure to follow your district's policy about communicating with the media.

5. *Build relationships.* The importance of building relationships has been emphasized throughout this book. There is no downside to building relationships but there is a tremendous upside. If principals have built solid relationships with people, they are less likely to have people view them negatively or question their motives. Therefore, less conflict is likely to occur.

Despite principals' efforts to avoid conflict, it still occurs. Here are some strategies to effectively resolve, or at least mitigate conflict when it happens.

How to Resolve Conflict When It Occurs

Although principals possess many attributes, they are not infallible. They sometimes make mistakes which result in conflict. When conflict occurs, there are several actions principals can take to mitigate it.

1. *Listen completely and genuinely to the concern.* When people are upset enough to call, write, or visit the principal with concerns, it behooves the principal to sincerely and completely listen to the issues. Stephen Covey (Covey 2005, 125) expressed this principle well when he stated, "Seek first to understand then to be understood." Here's how seeking first to understand, then to be understood can play out in practice. While the angry teacher, student, or parent is expressing, "Here is what I am upset about," the principal should demonstrate respect by:

- Actively listening rather than preparing your next answer
- Refraining from interrupting
- Asking clarifying questions
- Taking notes if needed—notes can help with getting the facts correct and then restating them
- Restating—"let me make sure I understand you"
- Listening for emotion and reflecting the emotion back
- Being sincere and empathetic—maintain eye contact
- Trying to determine what the person wants—if in doubt, ask

The principal might know how to resolve the issue before the angry person even fully presents it or shortly after understanding it. However, it is essential to listen completely, to withhold commenting or trying to solve the problem until the person has fully expressed the concern. Withholding comments makes a big deposit in the person's emotional bank account and causes the person to be more receptive to the forthcoming comments by the principal.

2. *Disagree without being disagreeable.* AFTER the principal has completely listened and confirmed understanding of the issue, then the principal can respond. Proverbs 15:1 says, "A gentle answer turns away wrath, but a harsh word stirs up anger." More than two thousand years later, that is still quite accurate and beneficial advice. A gentle, impassionate voice deescalates tension. A comment such as "I understand you but I don't agree with you" or "I understand you but I have a different perspective" in a monotone voice is a response that decreases, rather than increases, tension.

Such a comment may be the lead-in to the principal stating her or his viewpoint on the issue and finding a resolution to it. Principals' viewpoints or courses of action become more acceptable to critics if they can be backed up with some objective basis such as data or a school policy.

3. *Keep the focus on the issue rather than the other person's inappropriate behavior.* Angry or upset people sometimes behave badly and treat principals disrespectfully. Principals cannot respond with equally inappropriate behavior. If principals behave badly, then the focus of the conversation shifts from finding a solution to the issue to the bad behavior of the principal. Principals will quite likely be criticized if their behavior is questionable.

Sometimes, the person who brings the complaint or conflict to the principal is mistaken, and even though they were mistaken, they behaved badly when presenting the concern. How should a principal handle it when he or she is not only falsely accused but treated disrespectfully in the process?

Remember the importance of relationships and resist the urge to "put that person in their place." Principals may quite likely work for many more years with the teacher, student, or parent who was abusive, hostile, or illogical. Keeping a working relationship with them may be critical to one's daily peace of mind and success. It is better to build a bridge than to burn one. In such a case, principals can take the magnanimous approach of reminding the teacher of the mission of the school and their role in achieving it. Compliment their past contributions if possible.

Thank people for bringing the issue to your attention and mention that, if they were mistaken about the issue, maybe that means that you need to communicate better about it. Try to be an encourager even though it might be quite contrary to what you are thinking or feeling; keep building relationships.

4. *Be a role model at all times.* Just like in any other situation, the principal is a role model. That is an inherent responsibility and expectation of the position. Among other performance issues, principals should model expected behavior including excellent attendance, punctuality, proper planning, collegiality, respect for everyone, attention to detail, and avoidance of gossip.

Eleanor Roosevelt is reported to have said, "Great minds discuss ideas; average minds discuss events; small minds discuss people."[1] A principal who fails to be an exemplar of these characteristics is at a big disadvantage in eliciting them from his or her own staff. A principal's calm and composed demeanor when confronting conflict sets a positive example for students, staff, and parents. In addition to being unruffled, part of being a role model requires principals to be completely truthful and accurate in their responses.

What Should Principals Do If the Criticism of Them Is Accurate?

1. *Apologize.* When criticized, principals should assess whether there is any truth to the criticism. If there is, if their actions have caused the conflict, then they should apologize. People appreciate a leader who is big enough to admit that they made a mistake.

Apologizing for making a mistake which caused conflict is something that most people would naturally and logically do. But it is worth mentioning here because some principals think more highly of themselves than they do students, teachers, or parents. They might be inclined to use their positional power and be dismissive of the person who brings a complaint. Such pompous, arrogant behavior is likely to breed contempt. It is an action that destroys, rather than builds, relationships. If you make a mistake, own up to it.

2. *Rectify the situation and resolve to not make the same mistake twice.* If the principal caused the mistake, then it is their responsibility to rectify the situation. Ideally, the issue causing the present conflict can be resolved without further consequence. People make mistakes; we are all human. Principals, though, are often held to a standard of infallibility, even though they are quite fallible. That is why they must learn from their mistakes and the resultant conflict that those mistakes caused. Going forward, principals should implement protocols or other actions to ensure that the same mistake does not reoccur. Stay humble, teachable, and open to correction.

3. *Move on.* After apologizing and rectifying the situation, then principals should simply move on. Dwelling on the issue or beating oneself up for having made a mistake accomplishes little. Lesson learned. Go forward and keep doing good things.

Questions to Consider

1. What steps have I taken to avoid conflict in the first place?
2. Are there additional steps I should take?
3. When conflict occurs, am I skilled at resolving it?

4. What skills do I need to work on to improve my conflict resolution skills?
5. If my actions have caused conflict to occur, have I genuinely apologized and rectified the situation?
6. Do I need to implement any protocols or actions so that the same problem does not occur again?

References

Covey, S. (2005). *The seven habits of highly effective people.* London: Simon & Schuster.

Gratto, J. (2015, August). Addressing incivility in a civil manner. *School Administrator.* School Superintendents Association. Retrieved from https://aasa.org/content.aspx?id=37774.

Proverbs 15:1. Bible. New International Version.

Shaw, G. (2019). *7 Winning conflict resolution techniques: Master nonviolent and effective communication skills to resolve everyday conflicts in the workplace, relationships, marriage and crucial conversations.* US: Communication Excellence.

CHAPTER FOURTEEN

~

Friendly Advice

Ideas to Help Principals Personally and Professionally

> You are not here merely to make a living. You are here in order to enable the world to live more amply, with greater vision, with a finer spirit of hope and achievement. You are here to enrich the world, and you impoverish yourself if you forget the errand. (Woodrow Wilson)[1]

Throughout this book, many strategies have been offered to help prospective principals, and those already holding the position, master the intricacies of a very important job. But, there is more information related to the personal and professional attributes and actions necessary to make principals successful which don't fit so neatly into the previous chapters. After all, being a principal is a multifaceted job that requires one to be a master of many skills. As a wise, older, experienced, father gives advice to his son or daughter, this chapter is intended to share wisdom gained over the years. Collectively, the following compilation of ideas should enhance the skills of principals, thereby helping them to attain much success and flourish in the principalship. Here goes.

1. *A good name is rather to be chosen than great riches.* Many self-help books and personal improvement books take advice from biblical principles. This verse, Proverbs 22:1, is one of them. Although written thousands of years ago, it still has great relevance for today's leaders. Principals should continually strive to build a good name for themselves by being credible, consistent, honest, authentic, and diplomatically straightforward. Difficult times and questioning critics come with the territory of being a principal.

But principals who have built up a good name will weather those storms better than someone who has been inconsistent, disingenuous, or duplicitous in their actions.

2. *Don't get your honey where you get your money.* There are many people with whom a principal could be romantically involved. Students are definitely not among them. Getting involved in a relationship with students is against legal and moral norms. According to the Office for Civil Rights in the US Department of Education:

> With respect to sexual activity in particular, OCR will always view as unwelcome and nonconsensual, sexual activity between an adult school employee and . . . any student below the legal age of consent in his or her state. In cases involving a student who meets the legal age of consent in his or her state, there will still be a strong presumption that sexual activity between an adult school employee and a student is unwelcome and nonconsensual. (Title IX, A-6)

Getting involved in a relationship with a student is a surefire way to blow one's credibility, lose your license as a teacher and a principal, and quite likely do jail time.

Getting involved in a relationship with a staff member, particularly a subordinate, is not against the law but it may be contrary to school district policy. At the very least, it is unadvisable. Such a relationship could open up the principal to claims of favoritism toward the romantic partner. Real acts of favoritism could actually occur to the detriment of other staff members or students. Or, if the relationship goes south, it could open up the principal to claims of sexual harassment.

3. *Abstain from all appearance of evil* (1 Thessalonians 5:22), is another Bible verse that has significant implications for school leaders. The modern corollary of "Abstain from all appearance of evil" is, never do, say, or write anything that you would not want to appear on the front page of the newspaper. If our behavior gets us into trouble, words are not going to get us out of it. Principals have gotten themselves into trouble for changing grades, mishandling money, cursing at kids, looking at porn on their computers, and on and on.

Even if you don't do something illegal or contrary to school policy, you could still get yourself in trouble by doing something careless such as sending an inappropriate email. With the ease of sending off instantaneous but irretrievable emails, many principals have fallen prey to letting their guard down, sometimes with disastrous results. Whatever is written in an email could show up in thousands of inboxes or on the front page of a newspaper—sent there by the principal's detractors. Don't do such things or related foolish acts and don't even give the appearance that you are doing them.

4. *Procrastination is the thief of time.* There are so many demands upon principals' time that they cannot afford to procrastinate. Work put off doesn't go away; problems don't cure themselves when neglected. Rather than procrastinating, principals would serve themselves and their schools well by attending to issues promptly. Better yet, proactively plan to prevent as many problems as possible and to cause issues to go smoothly.

Take care of as many logistics as possible in the summer. Have a plan A, B, and C for as many issues as possible. You will certainly have to think on your feet every day. Preparation makes your job so much easier and increases your opportunities to delve into instructional practices and strategies to increase student learning.

Make a schedule of teacher observations. The main purpose of teacher evaluations is to provide constructive feedback to strengthen teachers' skills and effectiveness. If you wait and have to cram them in, they will not be genuine and you may miss good or bad educational practices happening in the classroom. So, schedule ample time for them. Observations put off are opportunities missed to improve teachers' and students' skills.

Take a notepad and pen or personal device with you when you go out into the hallway because you are likely to be asked five questions when you walk from point A to point B. Then, take care of those issues as promptly as possible. Doing so will enable you to handle them while they are fresh on your mind while being responsive to people. Practice "there is no time like the present" instead of "putting off until tomorrow."

There is a time, though, when procrastination may be helpful. That is when you don't have enough information to make an informed decision. In that case, it is wise to hold off on making decisions until sufficient information has been gathered to make a fully informed, prudent decision. That is especially true regarding important personnel decisions and student disciplinary decisions. In summary, don't procrastinate by putting off unpleasant or difficult work, but purposely hold off on decisions that require more information to resolve wisely.

5. *Live in the community where you are the principal.* This may be viewed as a controversial recommendation by some. Indeed, there are some bona fide reasons for not living in the community where one serves as the principal, namely greater privacy for the principal and their family. But, many people feel that the advantages of living in the community where one serves as the principal outweigh the disadvantages. When the principal lives in the

community and interacts with residents outside of school setting, these positive benefits occur:

- Confidence in the school increases as parents see that the principal has so much confidence in the school that they place their own children in the school.
- The principal can be responsive to parents' concerns when they encounter them in their ordinary activities.
- The principal can be viewed and known as a real person rather than just a person working for a paycheck.
- It will be easier to attend events. Attending events demonstrates interest in the school's activities and is also a great time to build relationships with parents and students.
- Commuting time can be minimized thus allowing the principal more down time or family time.

6. *Never let your supervisor or superintendent be surprised.* This point has been mentioned previously in this book but it is important enough to be mentioned again. Principals will sometimes be wrongly maligned by parents or teachers. They will sometimes be upset about something the principal may not be able to resolve or even by wise decisions, and they will bring their concern to the superintendent. Tell the superintendent the facts of the situation and your actions *before* the accuser gets there first.

Superintendents want principals to be successful and will typically act as the principal's ally. But, as was explained in the chapters about communicating effectively, people are unlikely to support something that they don't understand. Make sure the superintendent is well-informed about any issues that may reach his or her desk.

An easy and effective way for principals to keep the superintendent apprised of routine and upcoming issues and concerns is through a "Friday letter." Throughout the week the principal could write a paragraph or two about significant events as they occur. Then, on Friday afternoons before heading home, the principal could email the entire letter to the superintendent. That simple tool helps the superintendent to stay apprised of what is happening in the school and can reinforce the superintendent's confidence in the actions of the principal.

Confidence from the superintendent or direct supervisor matters. A superintendent is likely to gain trust and confidence in a principal who continually communicates positive accomplishments and the unvarnished truth about issues. At other times, principals may have to carry out directives that they don't entirely believe in from a superior. Having built a positive relationship and credibility with the superintendent by writing accurate Friday letters and communicating regularly, a principal who is respected by the superintendent is, therefore, in a position to state an argument for an alternative course of action.

7. *Communicate effectively with your colleagues.* In a school in which there is a principal and an assistant principal, both will handle many concerns throughout the day. These concerns will often carry over to the next day. One or the other may not be available to handle the concern when it pops back up because they are busy with a different issue. If the principal and assistant principal have taken the time to communicate effectively with each other, then either administrator can efficiently handle the issue.

Communicate with principal colleagues in other schools. It *is* lonely at the top. Sharing concerns and problem solving with collegial principals within the same school district or neighboring school systems can enable principals to solve problems more effectively while also providing some camaraderie and esprit de corps. In addition, don't be shy about asking for help. No one is going to expect you to know everything from day one, so do not be too proud to ask for advice and help when you need it. Even after you have been in the job for a while, you still won't know everything. Don't let pride get in the way of asking for help if you need it.

Develop a confidant, someone on your level, whom you trust and can share thoughts and feelings with. Be careful to problem solve, not whine or gossip.

8. *The principal is responsible for everything that happens in the school but doesn't have to do everything.* A sure way to become burned out is to try to attend to every detail, to be all things to all people, and try to be involved in everything that needs to be done. Delegate. Build the capacity of teachers and other school personnel to take on responsibilities. Help them as needed and trust people to get the job done. They may not complete tasks the way you would have done them but think deeply about whether that even matters.

It may be tempting and easy to assign tasks to outstanding teachers who always find a way to get the job done, who are highly regarded by their peers, or who go above and beyond their job role. Be careful not to go down the road of "No good deed goes unpunished." Don't make the lives of talented teachers miserable because they are good at what they do. Refrain from putting the most difficult students in their room, giving them inclusion for every block, or continually asking them to chair committees because you know they will do a good job with the assignment.

Doing so will contribute to their burnout rather than having them still be enthusiastic at the end of the year. Instead, keep cultivating leaders in the school by asking many people to take on responsibilities and helping them as needed.

Again, continually cultivate teacher-leaders, instructional leadership teams, and others who can make prudent decisions on your behalf. Such in-house leaders can become extensions of the principal and make the principal's life much easier.

9. *Continually build relationships.* The importance of building relationships has been mentioned a number of times throughout this book. Why mention it again? Because it is so important. There is no downside to building positive relationships with all staff members, students, and community members. Positive relationships built upon trust, transparency, and consistent actions become a valuable asset to principals when they have to make tough decisions.

Always remember that you are taking care of a parent's child. It is to be expected that parents advocate for the person they love the most in the world. Parents' opinions are valuable. Listen completely and genuinely to their concerns as described in the chapter on "Master communication and you manage conflict." Many times, parents just need to get something off of their chest. It's important to build relationships with them as well as with teachers, students, and support staff.

The more you are out of your office and in the hallways, classrooms, or lunchroom, the less discipline you will have to deal with. Be proactive. Similarly, build relationships with teachers by returning emails in person and practicing "management by walking around." At events, genuinely talk with students and parents. Find and create opportunities to continually build relationships.

10. *Don't shy away from difficult conversations and actions.* This topic was addressed in the chapter on "Motivating the unmotivated" but it is so important that it is worth reminding the reader of it again. As an example, many veteran principals and superintendents have likely asked themselves, "Who allowed this person to get tenure?" As mentioned previously, principals are held to a standard of infallibility even though they are quite fallible.

Is every single hire a good one or is it possible that some people who were hired should not have been? In many schools throughout the nation there are teachers or support staff members who simply are not good at their jobs or who mistreat students and fellow employees. Why are they still there? The answer could very well be that a principal(s) took the easy way out and avoided conflict. They gave teachers satisfactory evaluations or chose not to write up egregious behavior to avoid conflict. The result of such conflict-avoidance actions is that they allowed someone who was ill-suited for the position to remain in it.

Nobody likes difficult conversations and those attracted to the field of education are typically among those who *least* like difficult conversations. But, principals absolutely must rise above that tendency to avoid difficult conversations and be willing to discuss transgressions and document deficiencies in teachers' or staff members' performance. Such documentation can make the case for removing a substandard teacher (or other employee). Without such documentation of deficiencies, then it becomes very difficult for a principal or successor principal to remove a teacher.

When a new teacher is hired, relationships are at their friendliest and the principal wants that person to succeed. But principals need to guard against allowing that comfortable dynamic to restrict them from identifying deficiencies. Principals who find it hard to have difficult conversations should practice them by role-playing with other administrators. *It is a disservice to students, fellow employees, and the entire school to let inappropriate behavior occur simply because the principal chooses to avoid conflict rather than address deficient behavior.*

It is also wrong to use taxpayer dollars to pay someone for a job they are doing poorly and it's unfair and deflating to those who are doing their jobs properly. The job of the principal is to use all tools available to get unmotivated staff members to either meet performance standards or remove them from their position. Having difficult, courageous conversations is the first step in addressing inappropriate behavior.

11. *Make your personal wellness a top priority.* What is a synonym for principal? Problem solver. The job of a principal is quite demanding. It requires stamina and continual clarity of thought. Most days are long and require dozens of decisions to be made with a clear head. A principal's effectiveness can be enhanced if their physical, emotional, spiritual, and financial well-being is in good shape and their entire thought process is on the work of the school.

Conversely, if any of those areas are deficient, then the principal's effectiveness could be diminished because they are concentrating on a shortcoming in their overall wellness. Being entirely present on the job and being physically, emotionally, spiritually, and financially fit is not an either-or proposition. Principals should guard against the tendency to so immerse themselves in the job that they neglect their own wellness. They must find a balance between their work and developing all of the components of personal wellness if they are to be truly successful in their personal lives as well as on the job. With the proper mindset and determination backed by actions, both commitment to the job and personal wellness can be maintained.

Take time for yourself and your family, they are the people who will support you. If you don't, both your personal and professional life will suffer. Paperwork and responsibilities will always be there. Unfortunately, many principals have put their work ahead of their families. That can have tragic consequences. If you feel like your work and family life are out of balance, it may be worthwhile to read the chapter on "Maximizing the use of your time" again. Do not forsake your family for the sake of getting the job done.

12. *Remember that the principal is always a role model.* This point was also mentioned previously in this book but is significant enough to be emphasized again. Be humble and remember the bedrock principle of doing everything in the best interest of students. Be consistent in expectations and in your own everyday behavior, lead positive instructional change, and make school an enjoyable place to be.

Just as you would never want a teacher to say to a student, "Do this because I am the teacher and I told you so," don't tell a teacher, "Do this because I am the principal and you are not." There may be times when a directive approach is necessary, but generally speaking, don't let power go to your head. Think servant leadership. Convince people because of the power of your ideas rather than the power of your position. The chapter on "How would you like to have you as a principal?" noted that it is important to treat everyone with dignity and respect all the time. Follow the Golden Rule of treating others as you would want to be treated.

Get out of your office, walk around. Common gathering areas are a great place to build relationships with students. Be in the hallways, lunchroom, bus arrival and departure areas, and in classrooms. There should never be a time, in December, when you walk into a classroom and a student asks "who is that?" Show up in more places than Elvis.

When looking in the mirror every night, ask yourself, "Did I do everything in my power to make my school better today?" Effective role models pass the "mirror test" by answering "yes" to that question.

13. *Set yearly personal and professional improvement goals.* Continually improve your knowledge and skills. Read. Stay current on educational practices and philosophies. Not only will your knowledge and skills improve but teachers, your colleagues, and your superintendent will respect you for being an ongoing learner. Are there ways you could improve your personal life? You have challenged teachers by asking, "How good can this school be?"—ask yourself, "How good can I be?" PLAN challenging goals to improve yourself as a person and as principal. Remember, a goal is a dream with a date on it.

14. *Continually take actions to build an excellent school.* Only complying with state or district requirements has rarely, if ever, resulted in an outstanding school. Most people would consider mere compliance with requirements as a pretty low, uninspiring target. Doing what is expected or required is not exciting. Compliance does not inspire enthusiasm.

Striving for excellence inspires enthusiasm and motivation. Working hard to achieve a notable goal compels earnest action. Aim low, boring. Aim high, soaring. Principals should continually create and foster a culture that causes teachers to want to enthusiastically put forth their best effort every day so that students will achieve to their maximum ability. Furthermore, principals should continually encourage students to aim for excellence, to become all that they are capable of becoming, rather than merely aspiring to pass their courses.

This book cited a number of actions principals can take to build a school culture in which teachers and students strive for excellence. Undoubtedly there are more and although principals can be justifiably proud of the accomplishments of their school, they should never rest on their laurels. Instead, they should continually refine and improve upon every aspect of their school.

In the book, *Good to Great*, author Jim Collins says there was no "light-switch" moment where businesses all of a sudden were transformed from good businesses to great ones. Rather there was sustained, continuous improvement over a period of years that caused businesses to become great. "Good to great comes about by a cumulative process—step by step, action by action, decision by decision . . . that adds up to sustained and spectacular results (Collins 2001, 165). So it is with schools. Continual improvement will result in what others may view as an overnight success. But overnight successes don't happen. Principals control and lead continuous improvement efforts. Leave your school a better place than you found it.

In conjunction with the previous chapters, it is hoped that these bits of friendly advice help to prepare future principals to be highly effective and also to strengthen the skills of those people who are already principals. Being a principal is not the highest-paying job that someone could obtain, but it may be hard to find a job that is more significant or that has the potential to so positively impact so many students, teachers, and communities. The late teacher and astronaut, Christa McAuliffe, is credited with saying, "I touch the future. I teach."[2] That is an apt quote for those in the teaching profession.

This is an apropos quote for principals, "I shape the future. I lead." May the knowledge you have gained from this book enable you to shape a bright future for the school you lead.

References

Collins, J. (2001). *Good to great: Why some companies make the leap . . . and others don't*. New York: HarperCollins.

Gratto, J. (2005, June). Developing an action plan for wellness. *Councilgram* (newsletter for the New York State Council of School Superintendents).

———. (2014, December 11). The Friday letter: A powerful tool for keeping your board informed. AASA Executive Briefing.

———. (2011, November). Put down the damn fork. *Councilgram* (newsletter for the New York State Council of School Superintendents).

Proverbs 22:1. Bible. King James Version. Retrieved from https://www.biblegateway .com/passage/?search=Proverbs%2022%3A1&version=KJV.

1 Thessalonians 5:22. Bible. King James Version. Retrieved from https://www.bible gateway.com/passage/?search=1%20Thessalonians%205%3A22&version=KJV.

Title IX. United States Department of Education. Office for Civil Rights. Questions and answers on Title IX and sexual violence. Retrieved from http://www2.ed.gov/ about/offices/list/ocr/docs/qa-201404-title-ix.pdf.

~

Notes

Chapter 1

1. Haim Ginott quote retrieved from https://www.goodreads.com/quotes/81938-i -ve-come-to-a-frightening-conclusion-that-i-am-the.

Chapter 2

1. John Maxwell quote retrieved from https://addicted2success.com/quotes/50 -inspirational-john-maxwell-quotes/.

Chapter 3

1. Quoted from Kathryn R. Wentzel [and Jere Brophy (deceased)], *Motivating Students to Learn*, fourth edition (New York: Routledge, 2014).

2. Calvin Coolidge quotation retrieved from https://www.goodreads.com/quotes/ 2749-nothing-in-this-world-can-take-the-place-of-persistence.

Chapter 4

1. Walt Disney quote retrieved from https://signatureschoolproducts.com/blog/15 -quotes-for-educational-leadership/.

Chapter 5

1. Ron Edmunds quote retrieved from https://www.greatschoolspartnership.org/wp-content/uploads/2016/11/equity-quotes.pdf.

2. Henry Ford quote retrieved from https://www.brainyquote.com/search_results?q=henry+ford.

3. Confucius quote retrieved from https://www.brainyquote.com/quotes/confucius_140548.

Chapter 6

1. Margaret Mead quote retrieved from http://theperfectmeeting.com/resources/meeting-quotes/.

2. Dave Barry quote retrieved from http://theperfectmeeting.com/resources/meeting-quotes/.

Chapter 7

1. Arne Duncan quote retrieved from https://www.pinterest.com/pin/48202658482406540/.

Chapter 8

1. Bill Owens quote retrieved from https://www.inc.com/lolly-daskal/the-100-best-leadership-quotes-of-all-time.html.

Chapter 9

1. Remarks by the president on "My Brother's Keeper" initiative. (2014, February 27). The White House. Office of the Press Secretary. Retrieved from https://obamawhitehouse.archives.gov/the-press-office/2014/02/27/remarks-president-my-brothers-keeper-initiative.

Chapter 11

1. Victor Hugo quote retrieved from https://www.goodreads.com/quotes/271633-he-who-every-morning-plans-the-transaction-of-the-day.

Chapter 12

1. Quote from National School Public Relations Association (NSPRA), Professional Development, Communication Planning Resources, https://www.nspra.org/commplan.

Chapter 13

1. Eleanor Roosevelt quote retrieved from https://www.goalcast.com/2017/04/25/top-eleanor-roosevelt-quotes-inspire-greatness/.

Chapter 14

1. Woodrow Wilson quote retrieved from https://www.inc.com/lolly-daskal/the-100-best-leadership-quotes-of-all-time.html.

2. Christa McAuliffe quote retrieved from https://www.brainyquote.com/quotes/christa_mcauliffe_134582.

About the Author

John Gratto worked for six years as a physical education teacher and athletic director, five years as a K–12 principal, one year as an assistant superintendent for curriculum and instruction, and twenty-three years as a superintendent of schools in districts in New York State serving from 450 to 4,500 students.

Since 2012, he has served as an associate professor in the Educational Leadership program at Virginia Tech. He currently teaches graduate classes in Virginia Tech's principal preparation program—particularly Curriculum Leadership, Instructional Leadership, Personnel Administration, Leadership and Change, and Research, Assessment, and Evaluation—in addition to supervising teachers who are interning as principals. He also teaches "Administration of Instructional Programs" and "Governance and Policy" in Virginia Tech's doctoral program in Educational Leadership.

In 2001, he earned his EdD in education administration from Teachers College, Columbia University. He has authored a number of articles around the topics of helping principals, teachers, and students to be successful, board of education/superintendent relationships, wellness actions for administrators, and strategies to gain support for school budgets.

Dr. Gratto served as the president of the Virginia Professors of Educational Leadership from 2016–2020. He has also served as a member of the New York State Education Commissioner's Advisory Council, as a Blue Ribbon Schools Program review panelist for New York State elementary schools, as president of the Champlain Valley Athletic Conference, and as executive secretary of the Essex County School Boards Association.

When he is not teaching classes or reading, he is an avid bicyclist (having done many cross-state rides and an epic cross-country trip). His bicycle trips are accompanied by many ice cream stops. He also enjoys hiking and kayaking. Although he is much slower than he used to be, he also enjoys playing basketball. A history buff, he enjoys traveling to historical sites and national parks. Perhaps his biggest pastime in his free time is eating large quantities of chocolate.